THE AAA GUIDE TO BETTER ATHLETICS

Published in the same series by Pan Books

The PGA European Tour Guide to Better Golf
The LTA Guide to Better Tennis
The British Ski Federation Guide to Better Skiing
The SRA/WSRA Guide to Better Squash
The ASA Guide to Better Swimming

Forthcoming

The KUGB Guide to Better Karate
The Neil Adams Guide to Better Judo

THE AAA
GUIDE TO BETTER
ATHLETICS

Edited by Tony Ward

Photographs by Mark Shearman

A Pan Original

Pan Books
London, Sydney and Auckland

Contents

Steve Cram	*Foreword*	7
Mike Farrell	*Introduction*	9
Tony Ward	*Getting started: the basic route to success*	11

PART ONE — RUNNING

Linford Christie	*Sprints*	19
Todd Bennett	*400 metres*	29
David Moorcroft	*Middle-long distances*	37
Roger Hackney	*Steeplechase*	47

PART TWO — HURDLING

| **Mark Holtom** | *110 metres* | 55 |
| **David Hemery** | *400 metres* | 65 |

PART THREE — JUMPING AND VAULTING

| **Geoff Parsons** | *High jump* | 75 |
| **Lynn Davies** | *Long jump* | 85 |

| Andy Ashurst | *Pole vault* | 93 |
| John Herbert | *Triple jump* | 101 |

PART FOUR   THROWING

Geoff Capes	*Shot put*	111
Graham Savory	*Discus*	119
David Ottley	*Javelin*	127
David Smith	*Hammer*	135

PART FIVE   THE DECATHLON

| Eugene Gilkes | | 143 |

PART SIX   TIPS FROM THE TOP

Fatima Whitbread		153
Jack Buckner		154
Alan Pascoe		155
Roger Black		156
Michael McFarlane		157
Zola Budd		158

STEVE CRAM

Steve Cram is the European (twice) and
Commonwealth champion (twice) at
1500 m and the Commonwealth champion
at 800 m

Foreword

This book is a compendium of the wisdom of Britain's international athletes, all of whom have distinguished themselves at their particular event. It provides the sort of down-to-earth guidelines which have stood them in good stead throughout their careers.

A solid background with the correct technique and a positive, planned approach to training is paramount in achieving success in athletics. The message that comes across from each section is that you must find a good coach to guide you through the intricacies of preparation and competition. The relationship will change as the athlete matures, but it is special. As I can confirm, he or she remains a friend and a confidante for life.

Train hard and diligently, learn to deal with success and failure, and do not be daunted by apparent disaster: every career, no matter how great, has had its ups and downs.

Read every page of this book. There are 'track-wise' tips from every athlete which can apply across the whole spectrum of events that make up our sport.

British athletics rides high in world esteem at this time and I feel very privileged to have played a part in placing it there. The future prestige of our sport depends on our young talent and I know this book will help in setting many of them on the right path.

MIKE FARRELL

Mike Farrell is General Secretary of the Amateur Athletic Association

Introduction

It is a salient truth of the sport of athletics that the vast majority of athletes never come near to fulfilling their potential for a whole variety of reasons: lack of coaching; lack of adequate facilities (often in winter); lack of grit or determination in training or an inability to convert training potential into an equivalent competitive performance. Of course natural ability plays an important part in success in track and field, but proper channelling of that ability is essential for success to be achieved and that is where this book, full as it is of the wisdom of those who have 'made it' – in some cases to the very highest level – comes in. What we collectively hope to achieve is to point the way for fledgling athletes.

Finding the right club or coach, finding the best facility and getting down to the business of implementing a serious and planned training programme, are all down to the athlete. Much has been made over the years of the loneliness of the long-distance runner, but it is axiomatic. The lonely nights at track or gymnasium preparing the mind and body for the even lonelier moment of competitive truth are something that all serious athletes will experience.

Britain's prestige in track and field has never been higher. Each of our champions has ploughed a dedicated furrow to the top, each has competed at club and school level and each, I am sure, eagerly read books such as this in the beginning.

Three great distance runners: Cornelia Burki (Switzerland), Christina Boxer-Cahill (UK) and Mary Slaney (USA)

Getting Started: The Basic Route to Success

The majority of athletes belong to what I might call the 'What Shall We do Tonight?' school. They arrive at the track, clubhouse or sports hall, change, make a quick subjective judgement on their mental and physical well-being, look around to see what everyone else is doing and decide on some favourite or easy activity which they then undertake, often interspersed with long conversations with friends and acquaintances.

Now approaches to training depend very much upon the ambition of the athlete. For any athlete with a modicum of ambition such an approach is disastrous. And most athletes, as former European champion Bruce Tulloh once said, are looking for some means to improve their performance, preferably by the following Saturday. What has to be instilled – and this is the skill of most coaches – is a

(Left) Steve Ovett with coach Harry Wilson.

methodical approach, not only to training but to the whole of a serious athletics life. Often athletes are totally amazed at the improvement brought about after only a short time working under a coach, and it is safe to say that this is by working to a fairly strict regimen rather than by any magic properties the coach may possess. Trainers with wondrous massaging powers that could give a sprinter two yards and who haunt clubhouses are long since gone!

Athletes take stock very frequently, at the beginning of their career and at varying stages throughout. For the serious school athlete, ambitious to fulfil his or her potential, it is a vital exercise to undertake. If they are uncertain they should seek the advice of a parent or teacher, but the guidelines to be followed are quite straightforward. Making the correct decisions at the outset of a career is crucial. A wrong decision can waste two or three years or even ruin a whole career.

Tony Ward has been involved with a high level of athletics for twenty-five years. A former British senior coach, he is a frequent contributor to *Athletics Today*, *Running Magazine* and *Athletics Weekly*. He has also contributed to overseas publications. He is the author of *Modern Distance Running*, and with Denis Watts, *Athletics for the Seventies*. He is currently Public Relations Officer of the Amateur Athletics Association and the British Amateur Athletics Board.

THE CLUB

Choosing the right club within which to further one's career can make or break it. The fullest enquiries should be made about the clubs in the area – amongst fellow athletes, amongst officials. These should cover the following points:

1 *Training facilities* – are they adequate for that particular event; are there both outdoor and indoor training facilities; when are they available; is all equipment for the event readily available; is the track all-weather; is there a cooperative ground staff; when are the training days; can the training facility be used at any time; what are the charges.

2 *Competition* – does the club provide regular competition; does it compete in league competitions; is the required event adequately covered; is the required age group adequately covered; what is the cost to the athlete of attending home and away fixtures; what is the standard of other athletes in the relevant event and age group, i.e. will there be adequate competition; if the athlete is still at school, what is the club's attitude to potential clashes with school fixtures.

3 *Training nights* – are training nights well organized; is there an adequate coaching structure; how are new members received and welcomed; how long does it take for an athlete to become absorbed into club life; if the athlete already has a coach who does not belong to the club, will that coach be welcome on training nights; what are the hours of club training; how will the athlete travel to the training facility.

4 *Club life* – is there a good atmosphere at the club headquarters; does there appear to be a purpose about club activity; is there a good social programme; do the club officials appear positive and forward-looking; are there many athletes of his or her age group; does the club appear well-organized.

A good policy is to list your questions, then note down the answers and as the investigations proceed keep them in a plus or negative column. Whichever club comes out the best is the one to join, unless strong personal circumstances warrant otherwise. Each club should be visited on a training night. Athletes will soon discover what kind of organization they are contemplating. They should observe what is going on and not be afraid to ask pertinent questions. At the end of the day it should be remembered that their relationship with the club is always two-way. The club is there to serve them, to provide them with the necessary ingredients to service their careers; in return they are expected to contribute something to the club's life and reputation. (However, this can become difficult as the athlete reaches an increasingly higher standard, and often causes stresses and strains in club relationships.)

THE COACH

A few great athletes have made it on their own, but only a few. The vast majority have had the assistance of a coach or mentor somewhere along the way. Some partnerships have made athletics history, e.g. Dyson/Gardner; Cerutty/Elliott; Tellez/Lewis. In the technical events, working with a coach from the very beginning is paramount to success in achieving potential; even in the running events, the traditional world of the loner, learning and working to the basic fundamentals of a training programme can save much heartache later on. However, as much or even more care should be undertaken in finding the right coach as in finding the right club.

1   Qualifications?

Within the British Amateur Athletic Board coaching scheme there are a series of grades for coaches.
    (a)   Assistant club coach
    (b)   Club coach
    (c)   Senior coach
    (d)   Staff coach
    (e)   National event coach
    (f)   National coach
For (b) and (c) in this group, there are examinations; (d) and (e) are appointments and (f) are full-time professional coaches. The aspiring young athlete is most likely to come across the first three categories at a club or training track. Assistant club coaches are jacks-of-all-trades, often in the process of learning the art and science of coaching, and are ideal for group work – especially groups just entering the sport. What young athletes should

be on the lookout for is a specialist coach in their event. Do not be frightened to ask coaches if they are qualified. It will be taken as a sign of a serious approach on the athlete's part.

2   Personality

Coaches come with all personalities: authoritarian, democratic, easygoing, very demanding, extrovert, introvert and so on. There is no one coach to suit every athlete and it is very important to establish that coach and athlete will get on well together and that their personalities complement each other. Even schools' athletes will know what kind of coach they are looking for, because from their own school experience they will know that certain teachers brought out the best in them while others did not.

3   What size squad do they have?

This is important, because it will determine how much time the coach can devote to an athlete. Too large a squad will mean too much dissemination of a coach's time.

4   How many stars are there in their squad?

If a coach has a mega-star athlete or two or three internationals in the squad, then this may also severely detract from the time that they can devote to other athletes in the group.

5 How much time can the coach devote to the athlete?

Coaches do not have an infinite amount of time to devote to their charges, so it is important to ascertain at the outset just how often the athlete will be able to work with the coach. Daily supervision is not necessary and indeed is not even desirable.

To some this pre-appraisal of a coach may seem to border on the impertinent, but it must be remembered that any coach worth their salt is making a similar appraisal of the athlete: Are they likely to be dedicated? Are they worth my spending more of my valuable free time on? Can we work together? Are they ambitious? These are some of the questions that will be going through the coach's mind in the early stages of a partnership.

The athlete must remember that for the vast majority of club officials and club coaches, their activities are a labour of love. Not only do they receive no recompense for what they do, but they often spend fairly substantial sums in carrying out their work. This work must *never* be taken for granted.

SETTING TARGETS

Taking a long-term view is a very difficult business, for young athletes especially. Short-term success holds many attractions and with English Schools Championships, European Junior Championships and World Junior Championships now firmly in place on the calendar, international fame and success can come when quite young. However, success at European Junior Championships level does not necessarily guarantee equal success at the more senior European, World or Olympic level. On the one hand, proponents of a short-term view push for maximum success at the current age level of the athlete, letting future long-term development take care of itself. On the other hand is the coach who believes in a slow and steady build-up which hopefully will bring about senior success; this viewpoint can tend to fight shy of achieving short-term success. Both attitudes are wrong in my opinion. In the first instance, young athletes can burn themselves out – psychologically if not physically – with an intense training and competition regimen. There is also the problem of the transition from junior to senior level, which is often a far more difficult step mentally for the successful junior than for his more average peer. In the second instance, aiming at some far-distant athletic utopia is something which very few can achieve; you have to be of a very special temperament to sustain such motivation over a long period.

A third and successful approach is the one which has been adopted by many coach/athlete partnerships – most notably by Sebastian Coe and his father – of laying down an overall long-term plan with specific year-by-year targets and building steadily towards it. Short- and medium-term successes may well come along the way – Seb won a bronze medal in the 1978 European Junior Championships for example – and these will serve as motivation without detracting from the overall aims and objectives.

Kazimieirz Zimny (Poland) leads Britain's Derek Ibbotson in a three-mile race at the old White City stadium

KEEPING A RECORD

Keeping a record of training and performance serves as an invaluable guide. Most coaches insist on their charges doing so and it is a sound policy. What goes into the record very much depends on the relationship between athlete and coach and some may feel more comfortable keeping two records: one for general consumption, giving details of training and competition, plus physical and mental reactions to them which the coach will find valuable; and a second and more private diary recording personal details, thoughts and opinions, which can serve a useful purpose for the athlete alone.

Such records make comparisons – what kind of training was I attempting last year? what times was I recording? what poundage was I lifting? Seeing improvement marked down in black and white can provide great motivation. For the runner, the times achieved in time trials before important races again act as an excellent incentive. Secondly, and perhaps more valuably, the training logs serve as useful evidence when something is going wrong – poor performances, lethargy in training, niggling illnesses and injuries. A check on the previous weeks' and months' training can often highlight the reasons for such problems.

KEEPING FAITH

Keeping faith with one's coach and keeping faith with one's potential go hand in hand. The first nearly always stems from the second, and the world is littered with disappointed and often angry athletes who have failed to keep faith and have come to realize, much too late, what they might have been. Individual effort is paramount; if you are gifted in any sport, you should explore that gift to its utmost limits. Belief in one's potential often needs to be a stubborn belief, and is something that an athlete keeps deeply buried in the innermost depths of his soul. 'A man's reach', said Browning, 'must exceed his grasp, else what's a heaven for?'

USING THIS BOOK

What follows is the collective advice of a number of Britain's top international stars in their respective events. Their advice is not definitive – nothing is – but nevertheless will be instrumental in making the reader think about their approach to his or her event. The book should be read in its entirety, for the athlete will find hints and advice on training from all the internationals which apply across the board. There are not many schedules here, because schedules must be individual programmes put together by coach and athlete which fit into the lifestyle of the athlete, with all their specific needs and ambitions. Moreover, athletes should have a broad view of their sport. Make notes as you read and follow them up; underline what you feel is important – this should not be a pristine volume for a bookcase, but a working book. Our aim is that by the time you have finished, you as an athlete should know exactly where you are going.

Cooling off, the New York marathon

Part One: Running

LINFORD CHRISTIE

Linford Christie is the European 100 m champion and the European Indoor 200 m champion of 1986, and UK record holder at 100 m. He finished fourth in the 1987 World Championships

Sprints

You generally know from the word go whether or not you are a sprinter, for all those who have made the grade throughout the history of athletics have had basic, innate speed. Very rarely have distance runners or field event athletes discovered later in their careers that they have been sprinters all along – Allan Wells is a notable exception – whereas many who imagined they were sprinters have gone on to find out that they were better at another event. I discovered at around nine years of age that I was fairly good at sprinting, but even if you're sure of this, it is still best to try out other events when you are young.

Sprinters come in all shapes and sizes, though the most successful are at least 5'8" tall. To be successful you must be dedicated and not rely on your natural ability to get you through. The history of sprinting is littered with people unsuccessful because of this.

TECHNIQUE

Starting

It is very important to view the start as the first 30 metres of the race. So many youngsters consider the start to be solely what happens on the starting blocks; whereas what must be drilled into them is the pick-up towards full sprinting speed over the first third of the race. The sprinter must be drilled and drilled until his starting technique is second nature to him. For many years my start was the worst aspect of my racing simply because I was not well-drilled as a youngster. A really bad start can cost you the race, especially over 100 metres, so attention to this aspect of your running is vital.

From the moment the starter calls you to take your track suit off until you are running at full speed, one word should describe your attitude of mind – CONCENTRATION! A blink of an eyelid after the command 'Set' can lose you the race. Once you are called forward, your whole mind must be focused on the job in hand – getting away first. You will have ensured that your blocks are *firmly* in place by a few trial sprint starts.

THE START POSITION
Block spacing is a matter of comfort above all. The blocks also have to be spaced so that the most effective leg drive can be obtained. For instance, blocks which are too close together can cause too much strain on the arms and fingers, especially with starters who tend to hold in that position. On the command 'On Your Marks', you move ahead of the blocks and step back into them. The rule states that the toe of the spikes must touch the ground. On average the arms should be shoulder width apart, but again this will vary from athlete to athlete. The head should be in natural alignment with the body, so that you are looking forward 20 or 30 metres down the track.

SET
On the command 'Set', your hips move into their running position and your shoulders move slightly ahead of your hands. You are steadily poised and coiled like a spring waiting for the gun. Here there must be maximum concentration; the slightest inattention can lose the race.

THE GUN
On the gun, drive forward from the blocks. Here all concentration must be on 'keeping low' and this is where the month-after-month, year-after-year of starting drills should pay off. Many young sprinters immediately leap up into the normal running stance as soon as the gun is fired, which cuts down on their stride length – the sensation is almost like running on the spot – and thus valuable ground and hundredths of seconds are lost.

THE FIRST 30 METRES
At the gun, the lead arm is thrown forward and you aim at driving *forward*. Knee pick-up will take care of itself. Arm action throughout must concentrate on the *backward* pull, for this assists in leg drive. So, *pull the arm back* slightly bent and then get it forward as fast as possible to bring about the next pull back. The sprinter then *drives forward* and rises gradually over the first 30 metres to a full sprinting stance.

START DRILLS
The advice of a qualified coach is absolutely necessary in gaining a good sprint start and *this cannot be sought a moment too soon*. Many sprinters do not start being seriously coached until they are sixteen years of age and this is often too late – it certainly was in my case – for bad habits will almost certainly have set in by

Valeriy Borzov (USSR, centre), one of the world's greatest sprint technicians, shows tremendous knee lift early in a 100m heat. Far right is former 200m world record holder Pietro Mennea of Italy

then. Starting drills must be part of every training programme:

1 Always over at least 50 metres (the full bend for 200 metres).

2 Always against opposition. If others in the squad are slower than you, then give them a handicap.

Other activity such as uphill running *on grass* (never on the road), sometimes pulling a tyre, is ideal in order to train the body to *keep low* over the opening phase of the race.

STARTING FOR 200 METRES

At the start of the 200 metres the sprinter is on the bend but he should aim at the outset to achieve for himself as straight a line as is possible. So he will set his blocks on the outside of the lane, aiming at a starting 'line' tangential to the outside line of the lane inside him. Before the race you should stride the bend (tracks have different radii) and then you will discover the angle at which you will approach the bend and set your blocks accordingly. It is a general rule that the further out you are in lane terms from the inside of the track, the greater will be the angle of the blocks to the line inside you.

The aim in the 200 metres is to 'run a good bend', for invariably the athlete leading into the straight turns out to be the winner.

Relaxation

The key to great sprinting is relaxation. This applies to both sprint races, but especially to the 200 metres. Once an athlete begins to strain and tie-up, his shoulders rise, his head goes back and *he starts to slow down.* Maximum speed is reached at around 60 metres. So concentration (that word again) – on relaxing, keeping the knees high, swinging the arms back in a relaxed manner to keep the momentum going – is vitally important. If you get the opportunity of studying slow-motion film of great sprinting from the front, you will see just how relaxed they are. In the 200 metres this process has to apply for a much longer period – lactic acid and general fatigue are fighting to take over after 60 metres and your battle is as much if

not more with them than with the other sprinters!

In the longer race the sprinter in the lead has a big advantage, in that he can concentrate on relaxing and controlling the race whereas those behind him will tend to strain to catch up. If you are behind after the bend – like I am sometimes! – then the message is 'don't panic'. Panic creates strain and tension and you start to tie up. Just keep lifting your knees and concentrate on fast, relaxed sprinting.

It is a good maxim that the fitter you are, the more relaxed you can become.

The finish

The most important factor in finishing is that the sprinter should sprint for 110 metres or 210 metres; again this must be inculcated into the mind of the athlete. So many sprinters – even the most experienced – begin to anticipate the finish line about ten metres out and either start slowing down or begin to adopt a 'dip' finish, thus affecting their running action over the last four or five metres. Young and up-and-coming sprinters should first concentrate on sprinting *all the way through* the finish line and beyond.

Some sprinters do employ a dip finish (where the arms are thrown back and the trunk leaned excessively forward) which can win races in very close finishes. However, the timing of this technique is absolutely crucial if it is to be effective and requires constant practice. Unless a sprinter can perfect it, then he should just concentrate on maintaining good sprinting action through the line.

Ben Johnson (left) and Carl Lewis, rivals and supreme sprinters. Carl Lewis was the gold medallist for 100 m, 200 m, 4×100 m relay and long jump in the 1984 Los Angeles Olympics. In the 1987 World Championships, he was second to Ben Johnson's record-breaking run of 9.83 seconds. Johnson is famed for the incredible reaction and speed of his starts

Heats, semis and finals

A sprinter should not run faster than is absolutely necessary to qualify for a final. You not only need to save your supreme effort for the final, but it is also good tactics not to let the opposition know how well (or otherwise) you are going.

TRAINING

Winter

Winter training is the most important part of a sprinter's life. It is a truism that the harder you work in the winter, the easier it is in the summer. Not only do you gain in strength and stamina, it is also the time to try out experiments or introduce new ideas into training.

In the winter, sprinters should train over a series of distances right up to 400 metres. All running over 150, 200, 300 and 400 metres will be quality, with enough rest or walk-back in between to produce a similar run the next time around. This does not mean flat-out sprinting. The fastest I have ever run in training is 90 per cent – quite a lot is at 75 per cent. One good session that we do is 3×400 metres with a 6-minute recovery, but every week the 400 metre runs have to get faster. The general rule is to increase speed while keeping up the number of repetitions e.g. 6×150m; 4×200m; 3×300m – all at seven-eighths or so speed. The maxim is that when you train you should always feel that if you wanted to go faster, you could do so.

During the winter, three hard track sessions a week are enough for the young athlete, and one of these should be hill running on grass, about 60 metres, building up to ten repetitions with a walk down; this is a hard session. For all outdoor sessions in the bleakness of winter the athlete should equip himself with the most important piece of equipment he can have aside from his spikes – a pair of tights. I wear two pairs during the really cold weather.

Warming-up

My warm-up remains the same throughout the year. In the winter I wear a jog-suit and a wet-suit over my tights and vest. You cannot be too careful.

A good warm-up will take some 45 minutes. Jog two or three laps, follow with a session of about six strides and then go into a programme of stretching exercises. These are vitally important. One of the most important muscles in sprinting is the hamstring and it is the most vulnerable. The hamstrings must be stretched carefully and steadily. After the stretching, go into a set of drills which are important for every sprinter – high knee action, ankle exercise, bounding etc. Drills are introduced – and should be done religiously every day – as part of the maxim that practice makes perfect.

Weight training

I would not advise beginning until you are about sixteen years of age. *It must always be done under supervision.* My programme includes bench press, sit-ups, half-squats, military press, dumbell press and squats.

At the commencement of a weight training programme I do lots of repetitions with fairly light weights and then build up the poundage as the months go by.

A favourite exercise of mine is one that I learned from the great American sprinter Mel Lattany where I hold dumbells in either hand, stand with one foot in front of the other and then pump the arms in a sprinting action. I begin with twenty on each and then build up. Young athletes may well only start with a dumbell bar. Like all weight training exercises, this needs overall supervision.

Competitive season training

In general, an international athlete will begin competing later than his club compatriot because his major commitments – international championships etc. – come towards the end of the season. Younger athletes and school athletes always begin competing earlier, so their transition from winter to summer training will come earlier as well, usually around April.

As you enter the competitive season, everything gets faster. The distances in training reduce – probably never further than 200 metres – and you will not run so many repetitions. These get faster and there are longer rests in between them. It is a honing process of all the work that you have put in during the winter.

You are getting the speed back into your legs. At this time – and it is often an anxious one! – you are gauging how you are performing and this is where a training diary is of inestimable use. Details of every session, every time are faithfully recorded. A training diary enables you to make year-by-year comparisons. My coach keeps a record of every time-session that we do. Get a good coach and rely on him. He is the long-term planner.

Finally, enjoy your training. This is where group training can be so important for within a group, under a good coach, a good atmosphere can build up; you can relax and have a laugh, but still train very seriously.

PREPARING FOR RACES

On the day before a competition, do not become too friendly with those you are going to run against, or the aggression that you need will go. And aggression in sprinting is your explosion.

On the day of competition, once you begin warming up, talk to no one with the possible exception of your coach. This seclusion is vital for two reasons. First, if you start talking to everyone it can take away your concentration; second, if you begin chatting to other competitors inevitably sprint-times and best perform-ances (nearly always exaggerated!) are swapped and this can induce unnecessary anxiety.

Do not respect other people's times. Go out to a race resolved to do *your* best. Once you have made a race, or semi-final or a final, then you are as good as the next man. Think positively that you are as good as anyone in the field. If you let other people's performances get to you, then you will never make it. Go out there, have respect for yourself and do your own thing – that's how dreams are fulfilled.

On the gun, the first movement is from the hands and arms. The head still looks forward

The rear leg moves next, followed by the front leg.

Mid-stride phase into sprint action

The 'Set' position: the front leg is at approximately 90°, the rear at 70°. The arms are straight and the shoulders are as high as possible

Linford Christie practising starts at West London stadium. The 'On your marks' position. The blocks are set well back from the starting line. Arms are shoulder-width apart, the head is looking forward and the eyes are focused some 10m down the lane

The first stride almost complete: throughout, Linford keeps low, not rising too fast

A powerful drive from the right leg follows, with high knee lift. Positive arm action

Excellent extension of the rear (right) leg, giving maximum drive. Linford accelerates into a full sprint, continuing to display strong knee pick-up and a full range of arm movement

TODD BENNETT

Todd Bennett is the European Indoor 400 m champion of 1985 and 1987 and has won nine major championship medals at 200 m, 400 m and 4×400 m relay

400 Metres

Running the 400 metres is in fact controlled sprinting at something less than full speed, where distribution of effort and energy becomes vitally important. There are three obvious ways to tackle the distance.

1   Run a very fast first 200 m/300 m and then hang on, hoping that strength and fitness will carry you through. Many top athletes have tried this approach, always in the expectation that one day they will keep going and not 'die' over the final stages. The danger is obvious. Somewhere in the finishing straight, often at around 340 m, there is a 'brick wall' and when it is hit the oxygen debt can make finishing difficult. That slow-down, even if a big lead has been established, often gives the following runners a big incentive – we all like a hare to chase!

2   Run a slow first 200 m and then speed up over the second half of the race. This is frequently the tactic of one who is afraid of

Todd Bennett (left) anchoring the UK's successful 4×400 m relay against the USA at Gateshead International Stadium in 1986

the distance, or of sprinters who feel that sheer speed will carry them through in the latter stages. Again the dangers are only too obvious; it is difficult to achieve a real increase in speed over the second half of the race, while that exciting fast finish can frequently end with the runner still failing to catch the leaders.

3   Even or near-even pace running, which ideally means identical times for the first and second 200 m. In reality, even-pace running means a differential of at least a second. For instance, in the 1984 Los Angeles Olympics the Men's 400 m winner, Alonzo Babers (USA), ran 44.27 seconds. His 200 metre splits were 21.7 and 22.6 seconds, a differential of just 0.9 seconds. That is very close to even-pace running. It is interesting to note that Darren Clark (Australia), who finished fourth in the same race, ran 44.75 seconds with splits of 21.2 and 23.6 seconds – no comment is needed. This does however require both confidence and an ability to run one's own race irrespective of what may be happening with other runners over the first 300 metres.

Variations on those three themes are endless. With that in mind, two seconds could be seen as a reasonable differential figure to work for, with an athlete who is aiming for 50 seconds expecting to have splits of 24 and 26 seconds.

What, then, are the components of successful 400 m running? I would list them as follows:

(a) *Basic speed.* All the Olympic finalists in 1984 were capable of 20.8 seconds, or better, for the 200 m.

(b) *All-round background.* This involves

The superb world record holder Marita Koch (GDR), winner of twenty-one medals, sixteen of them gold at major championships

flexibility/mobility, general and elastic strength, anaerobic and aerobic work.

(c) *Judgement*. The 400 m runner must run in his own lane for the full distance and that means, if you are in the outside lane, seeing no one for the full distance. So the ability to go off fast enough and then to judge the pace and stick to it, is vital.

(d) *Courage*. Both mental and physical – training is tough, it often hurts and while racing can try one to the limit.

(e) *Ability to rise to the occasion*. This means turning in a top performance when it matters. There is little point in recording a personal best at an evening meeting with few timekeepers if you fail to make the County Championships a week later because you could not raise your performance. My clubmate at Team Solent, Roger

Black, is a wonderful example here; he won the European title and broke the British record in the same race.

Plan your training carefully. Never just do a session because others happen to be working to that pattern. A typical programme for the year could well be:

OCTOBER–DECEMBER
Principally conditioning work, as far as possible avoiding use of the track. Where possible make full use of indoor facilities for circuit training, weight training, hopping and bounding routines and mobility work. Outdoors, concentrate on fartlek running (interval training) in the early stages, followed by hill running and short recovery running over various distances on grass or any other suitable area.

JANUARY–MID-MARCH

The indoor work continues, but outdoors it is back to track work with a mix of sessions, e.g. 8×200m, 6×300m, pyramid sessions (100, 110, 120, 130, 140, 150 and back down) and occasional over-distance runs. One good testing session at this time of year is 500×400×300×200×100. All track sessions involve short recovery, while some technical skills elements are also included. Hill running and hopping/bounding are still important.

MID-MARCH–MAY

Ease out of the indoor sessions. On the track speed work becomes more intense, so gradually cut the number of runs, increase the recovery time and run faster. Typical sessions are 4×200, 4×300, 8×150. More technical work on aspects such as starting and bend running should be included.

JUNE–AUGUST

This is the height of the competitive season. Training becomes a sharpening and topping-up process with speed being the essential. This is best achieved by a limited number of fast runs with long recovery. Technical skills should still be worked on and there is need to devote some time to the mobility and flexibility aspects.

There is a lot in this programme, and many athletes will not have time to cover everything. The important thing is to plan your own programme, aiming at balance and variation. Never let your interest flag through sheer boredom with the routines you are following. Remember that there is a limit to what you can effectively com-

Never anticipate the finish, or success. Steve Heard dips to grab the race from an already celebratory Brian Whittle in an indoor match at Cosford

plete – over-training can turn out to be just as disastrous as not training at all.

My final advice is simple: ENJOY your athletics and never become obsessed with the sport. You cannot race 400m week after week and expect to do well, so try other distances, especially the shorter sprints. Remember, SPEED is the key.

PETER COE, SEBASTIAN COE'S COACH, COMMENTS:

Seb is shown at high speed in an 800m event: the arm action is thus at a sprinting pace.

The right leg is fully straight, and the powerful toe-off provides a strong drive right until the end of ground contact.

The leading leg changes. There is just the right degree of bend to minimise shock on ground contact and to avoid over-striding.

The leading leg changes again. Seb's full and regular regime of stretching and maximum mobility exercises is imperative for a wide range of movement around the hip joints.

The second support phase.

32

The support phase. The free leg shortens by folding. A tight fold brings the leg closer to the hip joint, thus speeding up the forward fling of the free leg.

The right knee rises high to facilitate the forward fling.

Throughout, the head is held high but beautifully balanced, thus reducing the strain on the neck muscles and giving a clear air passage for unrestricted breathing. Only a slight forward lean of the torso again indicates good hip mobility. Seb's fine muscular definition is a product of a carefully planned programme of strength training for speed.

Seb has a long stride for his height. If you compare him with Steve Ovett in stride for stride shots, you can see that despite significant differences in their physiques, they show great similarity in technique, the similarity of middle-distance men who can run fast quarters.

The action returns to its starting point.

HARRY WILSON, ZOLA BUDD'S COACH, COMMENTS:

Zola is shown running 1500 m

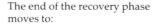

The end of the recovery phase moves to:

The support phase. In these two pictures, the right foot comes to the ground, the outer part of the ball of the foot striking the ground first, the heel lightly following. The 'flat-footed' position ensures the right leg supports the body while allowing the calf muscle a momentary rest. Arms are relaxed and in line with the body.

Zola keeps her feet and knees pointing straight to the front: all her drive is in a forward direction. As runners tire, the feet and knees can turn out, movement thus turning right and left and wasting momentum.

The left leg drives forward into:

The left leg folds up, the foot tucked close to the buttock, prior to swinging through. Body weight moves over in front of the right foot. The thigh lift of the now-leading left leg allows full extension. Great strength and mobility are vital for applying force and drive over a long distance. Arms, at approximately 90° angle, swing slightly across the body to enforce the forward thrust.

The ground-covering recovery phase

Throughout, like Seb Coe, Zola allows no energy-wasting tension in the neck and shoulder muscles. Her head remains steadily pointing forward. Her elbows do, however, tend to swing out, which can be problemmatical in a dense field

The recovery phase again

DAVID MOORCROFT

David Moorcroft was a Commonwealth champion at 1500 m (1978) and at 5000 m (1982) as well as a former world record holder for 5000 m

Middle-Long Distances

Britain has a proud tradition in the middle- and long-distance events. It is an area that provides a great challenge from a range of events.

Running these distances attracts people with very different physical attributes. Just compare Alberto Juantorena – the 6ft 2in Cuban who held the world record for 800 metres in 1977 with a time of 1.43.44 – with the 5ft 9in. Sebastian Coe who ran even faster, setting the current record of 1.41.73.

It also attracts those from a variety of backgrounds. The traditional introduction in Britain is through organized school cross-country, an activity which has discovered some of the greatest middle- and long-distance track talents in the world. Cross-country running is a demanding, tough sport, and it provides an ideal training for developing some of the attributes that make a successful runner. Mud, rain, wind and hills bring out the best in those individuals who are prepared to work very hard to attain their goals.

In recent years quite a number of middle- and long-distance runners have graduated through the ranks of sprinting. While coming up through the school and club junior ranks, athletes have found natural speed abilities may also be blessed with a capacity for endurance. Steve Ovett, a former English School 400 m winner, made the gradual transition through to an Olympic Gold medal at 800 m, world record 1500 m and mile and on to a Commonwealth Gold medal at 5000 m.

For many, running used to be something our teachers made us do when it was too wet to play football, or as a punishment for misbehaviour. It is no great surprise that many people disliked the activity and looked upon runners as rather eccentric individuals. And then came the 'run for fun' events like the *Sunday Times* Fun Run, the London Marathon and the Great North Run. Runners were everywhere, all ages and sizes, many battling against years of inactivity and others discovering a latent talent that they never knew they had.

RUNNING ACTION

In simple terms the ideal action is the one which gets you to the line quickest. There are no prizes for the most attractive stylist, but it is true that action can influence achievement.

There is a subtle difference between the efficient style and the attractive one. It is efficiency we are looking for and that varies between individuals and their event. There are, however, certain key elements and relaxation is one of them. Through the range of events the athlete needs to run smoothly with control and be relaxed. We all have our idiosyncrasies of style. These should not necessarily be discouraged, as they usually develop to aid balance even though the style may look clumsy. But beware bad habits; it is the responsibility of the coach to spot these and attempt to rectify them at an early age.

The head should be held relatively still. In particular, avoid the 'head back' problem which we often slip into when we are sprinting for the line. The 'rolling head' also comes into this category and, like the 'head back', is often a consequence of fatigue.

Tension in the shoulders, particularly towards the end of a race, often leads to the 'shoulders up' syndrome. This is one of my problems and again is a reaction to stress. As I get tired or when I am straining on the last lap of a race my shoulders and arms rise up, restricting full movement, and my style becomes less efficient.

Runners' arms are carried in a variety of equally effective ways during the race, and if it feels right a low arm carry or arms that carry across the body should not be a cause for concern. However, when the drive for the finish begins the classic arm pump action is desirable. Your coach can work on that aspect during specific technique work.

An exaggerated lean-forward or backward tendency should be avoided, and again this often becomes worse during the latter part of a race. Runners tend to be slightly round-shouldered and leaning forward a little is not a bad thing. It is over-lean that creates a problem.

From the hip and pelvis joints comes the all-important leg action. Over-rotation of the hip is inefficient, and the coach should be emphasizing the linear or straight line action as much as possible. Slight rotation is fairly natural, but effort spent swinging the hips around too much is effort wasted.

Knee lift, length of stride and foot plant are three contentious and often confusing points. In middle- and long-distance running we are in the compromise situation. Much of the race will be run with an economical style that develops naturally. The fitter you are and the less excess weight you carry, the more likely you are to run comfortably at a steady pace. World record holders who have shuffled quickly and Olympic champions who appear to over-stride contradict any hard and fast rule there may be on action.

Time should be spent throughout the year and at all stages of your running career doing some technique work. This is the opportunity to develop an effective style and concentrate on particular points away from the stress of competition.

A good running action has within it a range of movement that enables the runner to change pace at different stages in the race. It should be possible to adapt to

the environment, whether it be indoors, outdoors, track, road, on grass, on the flat or over barriers.

An efficient style becomes an effective one as a result of the all-important running ingredient – training.

A trio of Ethiopian runners: Kotu and Kedir are led by Yifter, Olympic champion in Moscow (1980) over 5000 m and 10,000 m

TRAINING

The range of events beginning with the 800 metres and going through to the marathon all require speed and endurance to varying degrees. In training terms these are developed through a variety of running sessions which can be categorized as predominantly aerobic or anaerobic.

Steady running allows the body to work relatively comfortably, the heart to pump powerfully and the exchanges of oxygen and carbon-dioxide through breathing to be in balance. If on a steady run you can chat quite comfortably to your partner, you can assume that you are working aerobically with an adequate supply of oxygen. Aerobic training can be defined as a 'chemical process in which oxygen is an essential part of the reaction'.

As the 800 metre runner reaches the bell he is probably going to be subjected to a last lap where a diminishing supply of oxygen will make fast running increasingly difficult. He will be forced to breathe at a faster rate and each breath will be shorter, his heartbeat will be high and the strength of each beat will be insufficient to distribute an already limited supply of oxygen through to the muscles. He is running anaerobically, he is shattered, he cannot run in this state for a very long time. Anaerobic running can be defined as a 'chemical process in which energy yielding activity occurs in the absence of or insufficient supply of oxygen'.

The three brilliant sportsmen who led the renaissance of British athletics in the eighties: Steve Ovett, Steve Cram and Sebastian Coe in the Olympic 1500 m in Moscow in 1980, won by Coe

Training sessions often contain a mixture of both states. It is convenient to put the 800 metre race at the anaerobic end, and the marathon at the other end as aerobic. We can then fit in the intermediate distances – 1500 m, 5000 m, steeplechase and 10,000 m – along the line. In reality, it is not this simple and the successful runner develops – between seasons and over the years – a high level of efficiency right through the range, and calls upon these abilities at different points in the event.

Young runners should be concerned about developing their speed abilities and not be in a hurry to move to longer distances. If the runner is taking part in school or club cross-country events in the winter, then training for that will provide an aerobic base. What often happens, though, is that the middle- and long-distance events are attractive because we feel we are not blessed with natural speed. Working on the ability to run fast is not an attempt to turn the runner into a sprinter; rather, it is to develop an important aspect of the runner's range of abilities. If this speed can be taken into the distance range, the athlete develops the ability to run in a steady state at a faster pace, and then possess a change of pace to use towards the end of a race when the fight for victory or a fast time is on.

As far as I am concerned, running fast is the basis of a training programme. Fast running can be over a range of distances from flat-out efforts of 50–100 metres, through repeat runs of 300, 400, 600 and 800 m distances and on to extended fast efforts for up to and over one mile.

When I was a youngster, my seasons

were quite separate. I concentrated on cross-country running during the winter, racing virtually every weekend, and in the summer ran the relatively short schools track season. As I got older I made the decision that track running would be my speciality, and as much as I enjoy cross-country running I now use that and the winter season as part of a planned build-up towards the track season. This is a fairly natural progression, but the early experience of regular varied competition was a perfect background and one that has nurtured most of the best middle- and long-distance talents Britain has produced.

The type of training and structure of the programme for a youngster should be seen

(Opposite) Mary Slaney (USA) wins the 1983 world 1500m title as the Soviet Union's Zaytseva falls just short of the line. A year later Slaney was to crash out in the Olympic 3000m

as part of a learning process, should be varied and fun and take into account the long-term development of the individual as well as the short-term aims of the coach, teacher, runner and his team. As the youngster matures and specializes, training becomes more specific. The overall combination of often twice-daily steady runs, further sessions and speed work prepares the athlete for the requirements of the chosen event.

SUMMARY

Success in middle- and long-distance running does not come overnight. The process of development is long-term and each season and year should be seen not in isolation, but as part of an overall, gradual build-up. Setbacks will happen; illness, injury and loss of form are all part of the process and learning to handle disappointment is integral.

Change occurs and one of the greatest things about running is that we reach our peak at different ages. Many so-called average runners develop with maturity into top-class athletes. Natural talent is only one of the ingredients of the successful runner; determination, application and patience are just as important. Most of us do not know or are not confident enough to believe how good we can become.

No matter at what level we are competing, we all share similar experiences of running. The satisfactions of improvement, of battling against the odds to overcome adversity and fulfil your ambitions, are a great motivation. With a modicum of talent, luck, ambition and hard work, the performance you achieve may be at the very highest level.

Cram smiles and Ovett gracefully acknowledges defeat in their epic race over one mile at Crystal Palace in 1983

(left) Ann Packer (UK) wins the Olympic 800 m in Tokyo, after only five 800 m races. She won silver at 400 m

The brilliant multi-distance runner, 1984 5000 m Olympic champion; 1987 world champion and current world record holder Said Aouita (Morocco)

(left) One of the greatest-ever milers, John Walker of New Zealand (right). Olympic champion in 1976; first man to run under 3:50 for the mile and first man to achieve 100 sub-four-minute miles

DR ROGER HACKNEY

Roger Hackney was the 1986 Commonwealth silver medallist at steeplechase and was fifth in the World Championships of 1983

Steeplechase

The steeplechase is a middle-distance event with the added excitement of four barriers and a water jump per lap. Senior men race over 3,000 metres, Juniors over 2,000 metres and Youths over 1,500 metres.

The event is gruelling, with unique requirements of endurance, strength, speed and skill. Its origins are old. Together with the sport of cross-country, steeplechasing descended from the ancient practice of running races between church steeples, village to village. These races took place as the crow flies, with hedges and ditches to be crossed.

APPROACHING THE EVENT

If one wants to specialize, it is important always to keep in mind that the steeplechase is essentially a middle-distance race. So what differences does a runner find in a race 'over the sticks' as compared with a 3,000 metres flat race? Without specific preparation, he will find that on approaching a barrier he will misjudge his take-off point, jump too high over the hurdle, be off-balance on landing and once the barrier has been negotiated, will find that he has slowed down so that he has to accelerate hard to catch up with the opposition. Spectators will see that his rhythm has been disrupted. When he gets to the water jump he will expend a great deal of energy and jar his legs badly on landing – as well as getting wet! The unfortunate runner will feel as though he has just run a 1,500 metre race only to find that he has, in fact, to keep going for 5,000 metres. Nobody told him, either, that the barriers seemingly got higher the further he went.

Many talented runners have tried to make a name for themselves by gaining what they thought would be an easy selection for a major championship at the steeplechase, only to find themselves beaten by runners they probably thought less talented than themselves. Being a good middle-distance runner is not enough. Preparation is specific and very important. If you watch an Olympic steeplechase final, you will see that the athletes flow over the barriers as if they were hardly there.

TECHNIQUE

The 'novice steeplechaser' to whom we just referred encountered a number of problems. As he approached the barrier he slowed down and shuffled his feet, trying to decide which leg to jump with. Sighting the barrier is difficult, perhaps the most important and yet the most awkward aspect of the skill of hurdling. Practice is vital throughout the whole year. My tip is that when out on normal training runs you should learn to look for a mark some 15–20 metres away and put your foot on it, just as if it was the point you would jump from to clear a hurdle. Try to do this with as little alteration in stride as possible.

Negotiating the barrier from take-off requires a degree of flexibility usually

Good hurdling technique is fundamental to steeplechasing. Henry Marsh (number 919) of the USA displays technique that would grace a 400 m hurdler. In the middle is Colin Reitz of Great Britain, and on the right the Olympic champion Julius Korir (586) of Kenya

absent in a middle-distance runner. My basic advice to potential steeplechasers is to train to be able to stretch and be mobile enough to achieve the 'hurdle' position – that is, leading leg straight on the ground, trunk upright, trail leg at 90 degrees to both, with the knee of the trail leg at 90 degrees flexion.

Once this position can be achieved comfortably, the hurdler will not need to jump so high and will be more balanced throughout his hurdle action and on landing. *Economy* is the keyword in hurdling for the steeplechase. Steeplechasers should flow and maintain the rhythm with sudden acceleration; the emphasis here is on conserving energy.

THE WATER JUMP

The water jump is an obstacle unique to the event. The barrier is the standard height, but there is a lot of water to negotiate. I do not recommend that anyone tries to clear the water fully!

Once more *economy* is the watchword, with the aim of not breaking rhythm, jumping as low as possible on to the barrier in order to conserve energy. The lead leg lands with the spike plate able to roll over the barrier and on to the opposite edge. The athlete should aim to keep his bottom as low as possible over the barrier, swinging the trail leg under. As the trail leg is brought through, the lead leg straightens and remains on the barrier. The trail, *now leading leg*, reaches towards the water's edge, landing at ankle-depth. Leaving the leading leg on the barrier as long as is possible allows the first stride away from the water to be a good length. There is no need to actively push from the barrier, as there is sufficient speed to carry you through.

Mistakes commonly arise from a poor take-off position. Being too far away from the barrier leads to forward rotation, corrected by jumping hard off the top of the barrier – a great waste of energy. If you take off too closely, then this will lead to continued upward flight, reducing forward momentum and ending in a heavy landing in deep water!

When approaching the jump, it is really very important to be able to judge your own stride length and to make a single adjustment if necessary. I do not believe in marking the track with take-off points, because in bigger competitions this is impractical. There is no substitute for rehearsal in training.

Generally, athletes have a dominant lead leg. In championship races, however, sighting the obstacle may be very late. Other runners may be obscuring your view. It is then extremely useful to hurdle with either leg as lead; this needs practice and training, with stretching and drills.

Water jump clearance at the Moscow Olympics, 1980. Note how the athletes do not attempt fully to clear the water, and how they run forcefully away from the water jump

TRAINING

In writing about middle-long distances (see p.37), David Moorcroft has fully covered the kind of running/training programme required for the steeplechase. You should read his section in full, noting that training for steeplechasing should be pitched between that for 1,500 metres and for 5,000 metres, and a good steeplechaser will be able to run both distances well. However, I do not consider that there should be a bias to either of these distance events. Bronislaw Malinowski, the Polish 1980 Olympic champion, had run 3 mins. 37 secs. for 1,500 metres, but also achieved some fast 10,000 metre races and finished second in the World Cross-Country Championships in Limerick. Henry Rono, the current world record holder, has also held records from 3,000 metres to 10,000 metres. You might think that height is an advantage, but Henry Rono, Patrick Ilg, the 1983 World Champion, Henry Marsh and Julius Korir – the 1984 Olympic champion – are all comparatively short.

You should also absorb the hurdle drills put forward by Mark Holtom and David Hemery. In the winter, make a daily habit of putting out three or four sprint hurdles at the correct height and going through some drills as part of your warm-up. Place a steeplechase hurdle in front of a long-jump pit and practise a dozen jumps. Use an observer to correct any technical errors.

The steeplechase is a tough event without the glamour of the mile. Yet it can be the most exciting of races to run or to watch. Remember the drama of Henry Marsh falling at the last barrier at the World Championships in Helsinki in 1983, or Filbert Bayi in the Moscow Olympics setting off far to fast and being caught by Malinowski on the last lap. I find it a fascinating and very rewarding event.

Colin Reitz (5) of Great Britain ahead of Joseph Mahmoud of France

WATER JUMP TRAINING USING A STANDARD BARRIER AND

The trail leg is brought through

Aim to put the lead foot on to the barrier so that the front of the spike plate rolls over to the opposite side. Note the right thigh is horizontal and the body is flexed forward so the shoulders are as low as possible, saving energy

The left leg bends to absorb the shock of landing: the next stride away is a good length and a continuation of normal running action

The right leg swings through: the athlete lands on one foot, on the same spot as on a previous jump. It is important to perfect technique, and use it without thinking

SAND PIT TO MINIMIZE INJURY

The take-off, an exaggeration of normal running action. Running momentum should be sufficient to carry the athlete through

Take-off point, 2–3 m before the jump

The approach: any adjustment in stride length should be made 20 m before the barrier

The trunk straightens, and the lead leg reaches towards the 'water's' edge. The athlete is balanced with a good stretch

The lead foot gives a gentle push off, and is left on the barrier as long as possible to counteract forward rotation

Part Two: Hurdling

MARK HOLTOM

Mark Holtom was a Commonwealth champion at 110 m hurdles and former UK record holder

110 metres

In recent years the shorter hurdle events have been referred to as 'sprint hurdles', and this trend indicates the main requirement for success – SPEED! Naturally, the obstacles have to be cleared as efficiently as possible with a minimal interruption of an athlete's sprinting speed. Therefore in order to achieve the maximum efficiency, an athlete must practise running over hurdles again and again until the clearance becomes almost second-nature.

Not so long ago, hurdlers were chosen because they could sit on the ground in the so-called 'hurdling position', and if they were tall and long-legged then these were further bonuses. However, today's sprint hurdlers come in a variety of sizes, though the two main advantages are the ability to move one's limbs quickly and the length of leg in relation to the body. From an early stage the athlete must dismiss the idea of 'jumping' over hurdles and get used to 'running over' them as quickly as possible.

TECHNIQUE

Essentially, you grasp the basics at a speed you can control and then move more quickly as you become more confident and proficient. At high speed it only takes one mistake for disaster to occur, and if disasters happen in hurdle races it usually indicates that the athlete has not worked hard enough in preparing for all parts of the race.

There are four distinct phases in sprint hurdling: the start, hurdle clearance, running between the hurdles and the finish.

Each of these phases must be practised individually in training, but the hurdler must always remember the need to put the phases together and practise the whole concept of hurdling.

The start

Controlled speed is the main requirement of a start in a hurdles race, because the need to get away as quickly as possible is tempered by the presence of a hurdle after seven or eight strides. Too many young athletes waste time by trying to use a crouch start or starting-blocks too soon. It is best to use a standing start in a comfortable position and develop a consistent stride-pattern to the first hurdle. Athletes have to experiment to find the most natural position at the start so as to reach the hurdle on their better leg.

When eight strides are used to the first hurdle, the first three strides must be fast and constant, the arm action is important in determining the speed of the legs. After the initial momentum gained on the first three strides, the hurdler must come into an upright sprinting position by the sixth stride in order to sight the hurdle properly. Any adjustment will be made on the last two strides before the actual clearance.

Hurdlers must practise their start over hurdles, and if they are also competing in sprint races, they must understand the separate requirements of each. Sprinters do not get into their upright sprinting until somewhere around 25 metres, but hurdlers will find they have a hurdle to clear after about 12 metres and if they are not

ready for it, the first mistake will be made at a very early stage of the race. The importance of reaching this first hurdle quickly and clearing it successfully can be stressed by the fact that the approach to the first hurdle is the longest part of the race without an obstacle to be cleared.

Hurdle clearance

Early hurdle races were held over very substantial barriers such as rustic fencing. The emphasis was very much on *clearance*, though even with today's modern hurdles there cannot be a hurdler who has not experienced pain and injury caused by an imperfect clearance.

Athletes must approach the hurdle running on their toes and without any lowering of the hips so that they can dominate the hurdle. As with sprinting, the first movement is an explosive lifting of the leading knee towards the hurdle barrier with the foot held back as long as possible. After this first movement the athlete will drive the lower part of the leg at the hurdle-rail. Once it has been crossed, the third movement of this leg will bring the athlete on to the ground as soon as possible. It is important to remember that time in the air is time wasted, because you cannot run in the air.

While the lead leg must be moved quickly and aggressively, the other leg aims for balance and efficiency. Harmony of movement between the two legs is the most important thing, and the thigh of the trailing leg must aim to cross the hurdle-rail in a position parallel to the ground. A fluent movement is necessary, and the

One of the all-time greats, 1983 and 1987 world champion Greg Foster (USA)

lower part of the leg remains as close to the calf as possible. As soon as the hurdle-rail is crossed, the thigh moves forward and the foot begins to reach for the first stride away from the hurdle. If the knee drops too soon the hurdle will be hit and speed will be lost; another very common fault is for the toe of the trailing foot to point at the floor and hook the hurdle on its way across; again, constant practice under supervision is essential for these points to be fully rehearsed.

Drive across the hurdle will be improved if the athlete leans his whole trunk at the hurdle, remembering to keep his hips and shoulders moving forward at all times. An over-exaggerated body-lean can be just as counter-productive as an upright posture over the hurdle. But in general terms, the higher the hurdle or the shorter the athlete, the more pronounced the body-lean will be.

The athlete's arms will be moved in opposite phase to the legs. Their movement will be as natural as possible, their main function being to maintain balance and correct mistakes in much the same way as a skier uses his ski-poles. The main point of emphasis is for the opposite arm to be thrust forward at the same time as the leading leg at shoulder's width apart; do not try to touch your toe in mid-air because this will result in a loss of momentum and balance.

Running between the hurdles

In the three running strides between each hurdle, the athlete has to regain balance after crossing the hurdle, run as quickly as possible and set himself up for the next clearance. The maintainance of running speed requires a considerable amount of skill and rhythm. There should be a measured fluency throughout your movements. The athlete must run off each hurdle with an emphasis on aggressive arm movement and there must be no lowering of the hips. Ragged technique will limit the speed between the hurdles, and similarly slow running will limit the technical efficiency of the clearance.

The finish

Over the last few strides (usually 5 or 6) the athlete becomes a sprinter again; at every level, hurdle races are often won or lost on the run-in. It is vital to sprint off the last hurdle and to time the dip for the line to perfection; many athletes dip too soon and this reduces speed at a critical moment. Most successful hurdlers practise sprinting off the last hurdle in training whether it is the second hurdle or the tenth, because finishing habits can be ingrained throughout training.

In order to achieve their goal athletes must:

(a) start properly to the first hurdle,
(b) clear each hurdle efficiently,
(c) run between each of the hurdles quickly; and
(d) run off the last hurdle and finish.

World record holder Renaldo Nehemiah of the USA

Aggressive hurdling by Britain's 1987 world silver medallist Jon Ridgeon at Cosford. Note how he is skimming the hurdle

TRAINING

In the winter months the foundations will be laid; in the spring the emphasis will switch from quantity to quality; and the summer months will be geared towards competition and more intensive work with an objective in mind. Both training sessions and competition should have a definite aim. Training for the sake of it or to relieve boredom will achieve little, and its value is questionable.

When working out which training sessions will be the most useful for the sprint hurdles event, the athlete must take time to look at the following:

1 *How much time is available for sessions?* Inevitably this will take into consideration factors such as school, work, home, social life, other interests, etc.

2 *What facilities are available?* Some of the sessions require special apparatus like multi-gyms or indoor areas to practise hurdling in adverse weather conditions.

3 *How often can the athlete do a session with a coach or teacher?* Some training can be done individually or with a group of other athletes if the motivation exists in the first place, but all hurdling sessions will benefit from 'a second pair of eyes'.

4 *What sessions will help individual athletes overcome their weaknesses and become successful sprint hurdlers?* It is essential to think most carefully about the demands of sprint hurdling and consider which activities will help development as a hurdler.

Training can become tedious if sessions are identical, and as the athlete becomes more experienced variety is as essential as gradual progression. The following list of the requirements of the event and the type of training necessary will be useful to the young hurdler.

Hurdling

Hurdlers need to practise the skill of hurdling as often as possible. In training the whole event must be practised, and as there are either 8 or 10 hurdles in a race, the successful hurdler will run over the full distance.

Hurdle races take place in all kinds of climatic conditions, and the winds may be helpful or unhelpful. Therefore these conditions must be reproduced in training, and some runs must be made into the wind. The only restriction on hurdle practice comes when conditions are dangerous. Do not hurdle on wet or uneven grass surfaces, and make sure that all the hurdles are positioned so that they fall away from the athlete.

Running

The majority of training sessions will involve running, but many hurdlers warm up for these by performing some of the skill work over hurdles in the same way as they would prepare for a hurdle race. Some of the running will be aimed at improving the general condition of the athlete; the runs will not be flat out, there will be a lot of them and greater distances will be covered. As the season approaches and the athlete looks for more speed, the runs will become faster, there will be fewer of them, the distances will be shorter and the recovery between runs will be greater.

Strength

Hurdling is an explosive event, therefore sprint hurdlers must have sufficient strength for it. Experienced athletes will spend a proportion of their training time in the weights room or on a multi- gym, but these pieces of apparatus require separate skills and beginners would be better advised to develop their strength in other ways. Circuit training is an excellent way, using an athlete's body weight or simple apparatus; the exercises are many and varied, and athletes can work in groups. Some hurdlers use bounding and hopping on dry, flat surfaces; this will improve explosive strength, but the correct technique is important. So is the right footwear – training shoes with a good heel wedge. However, one of the best ways for a sprint hurdler to develop the right kind of strength for the event is hill-running. The length and the gradient of the hill will help in conditioning and explosive strength, but if the emphasis is placed on running on the toes, high knee-lift and no lowering of the hips when running up the hill, then the three main requirements of hurdling will benefit.

Mobility

Hurdlers tend to be relatively mobile athletes, but they must not neglect exercises which will increase the range of movement in their limbs. The clearance itself is not a natural movement and athletes must pay regular attention to ensure a sufficient range of movement in both hips. Never confuse mobility with suppleness. The latter comes from stretching the muscle groups in the warm-up for every session, and hurdlers neglect to do this at their peril.

CONCLUSION

The hurdles is the most technically demanding event in athletics. There are no short cuts to success. Sprint hurdling demands commitment from the athlete and the patience to develop the necessary skill at speed over a long period of time.

(Opposite) 1986 world junior champion and 1987 world bronze medallist Colin Jackson (UK)

Class	Length of race	No. of hurdles	Approach	Hurdle interval
Junior Boys	80m	8 @ 84cm	12m	8m
Youths	100m	10 @ 91cm	13m	8.5m
Junior Men	110m	10 @ 99cm	13.72m	9.14m
Seniors	110m	10 @ 106cm	13.72m	9.14m
Junior Girls	75m	8 @ 76cm	11.5m	7.5m
Intermediates	80m	8 @ 76cm	12m	8m
Euro-Juniors	100m	10 @ 84cm	13m	8.5m
Seniors	100m	10 @ 84cm	13m	8.5m

JON RIDGEON TRAINING AT CRYSTAL PALACE

Jon approaches the hurdle: good sprinting action is vital

The start of the action over the hurdle. The right arm drives forward

Note the high leg follow-through, so that Jon can get straight into sprinting again

Fast knee pick-up at the hurdle: right arm is thrown forward and slightly across

Good body lean, with the heel of the front leg leading across. The rear leg is bending sideways to clear

Excellent hurdle action: the athlete's rear leg is just skimming the barrier

Sprinting away from the hurdle. Note again good sprint technique – positive arm action and high knee lift

DAVID HEMERY

David Hemery was the 1968 Olympic 400 m hurdles champion and set a world record in that race

400 Metres

400 metre hurdling involves clearing ten hurdles spaced every thirty-five metres around the track. With that amount of distance to cover between hurdles, there is quite a variety of strides taken between each. When counting strides, don't count the landing foot; the follow-up step is the first. The least number of strides currently used is thirteen between each barrier by Edwin Moses. Most international women start with fifteen strides between each hurdle. The number taken by a young athlete will vary according to their strength and size. Even at senior age level, the strides at the end of a race may be anything from fifteen to twenty; but obviously, the fewer strides taken the better, as long as speed is maintained with a good stride length. The reason why hurdlers are unable to maintain the same stride pattern throughout the race is because fatigue forces their stride length to decrease. The athlete is eventually too far from the next hurdle to clear it and must either take off from the other foot or put in an extra stride or two. Learning to count strides while running helps you concentrate on maintaining a decent stride pattern.

It is important to establish rhythm and flow and in order to do that, two things are necessary. First, the athlete must hurdle frequently enough to be capable of adjusting stride length some distance from each hurdle. (Stutter stepping right before a hurdle will not only kill momentum but also waste energy in re-establishing speed.) Second, they must be fit enough to maintain a reasonable speed and rhythm throughout the race.

TECHNIQUE

In introducing the hurdling action, the first aspect to establish is that it is a driving push out, rather than up. This point can be made by placing a couple of towels on the track and having the athlete long stride over them. The next step is to have some very low objects which will fall easily if knocked; miniature hurdles are ideal. These should be placed at regular intervals so that the athlete can become familiar with the rhythm of hurdling. Then increase the height by doubling up the mini-hurdles or whatever else is being used. The athlete must build up confidence in clearing a barrier without bruising a knee. The next aspect is to ensure that the athlete is still pushing off hard. I recommend placing one hurdle behind another.

For goodness' sake, don't hit them! Start

by having them very low and take off from a good footing.

The start

A good first hurdle clearance is almost as important to the 400m hurdler as to the sprint hurdler. Practice starts should always be over more than one hurdle to establish the speed and rhythm of the race.

Balance

Good hurdle clearance is established at take-off. Hurdlers should think of themselves as running on a tightrope and deviate as little as possible from the straight line. Any off-balance motion can result in loss of time; therefore every action should be controlled.

The lead leg

The lead leg is the leg lifted over the hurdle first. The drive over the hurdle should be initiated with a high and fast knee lift; the lower leg is held back. The foot of the lead leg has the toe up, but is not swung forward until the knee has reached its highest point. From that point the heel of the lead leg is pushed straight out, as hard as possible, just above the height of the hurdle. Aim your heel a couple of inches to the left or right of centre, depending on which is your lead leg. A common fault is allowing the lower leg to deviate below the knee from a straight lift and extension; it is left circling towards the outside of the hur-

dles or, if the athlete takes off close to the hurdle, the lower leg is bent under the runner and hooked over the hurdle.

Landing

On landing your lead leg should be pulled down to the ground under you. This means work for the hamstring (back of the thigh) muscle. You should land on the ball of your foot, attempting to stay as tall as possible, not allowing the knee to bend on landing. The lead leg is the landing leg and should be considered as a pivot. The hamstring should be working hard to pull the body into the next stride, but if the landing position is correct you land with most of your body weight directly over the foot. Bending the landing leg can result in a considerable loss of momentum.

The lead arm

For the sake of illustration, take the left leg as the lead leg. The athlete's right hand and arm must balance this exaggerated knee lift. The elbow should be lifted up to shoulder height and as the foot is driven over the top of the hurdle, the hand is extended towards that foot. Very briefly the hand is held out there before coming back around the trail or take-off leg. The return route of the lead arm is vital for good balance, and it should not be swung back too early. The arm action is very similar to pulling water around oneself in a bath. The elbow must remain high and slightly bent (90–120 degrees). The hand

Harald Schmid (Federal Republic of Germany), winner of five European gold medals, three for 400 m hurdles, showing a fluid technique

must be lower than the elbow and is swept around the knee. The arm remaining slightly bent should prevent the hand from swinging wildly behind, which often results in the hurdler swinging off-balance for a stride or two.

The shoulders

The shoulders should be kept as square as possible. At take-off there should be a leaning of the chest towards the centre of the hurdle. This does not mean a torso twist, simply that the lead arm is stretched out and the opposite arm is drawn back; the hand of the lead arm has the palm facing down. The other arm should be held back at approximately 90 degrees. With the palm down, that hand is held close to the body at about the level of a trouser pocket; it is then in a good position to drive up in good sprint form on the follow-up stride after landing.

The trail leg

The trail leg is the one which is used to drive off the ground. That push-off should

67

be done with the greatest force possible. The toe is turned out and held up, Charlie Chaplin style, after take-off; this will cause the knee to come around to the side, but the main thought should be to lift the knee around to the straight line of sprinting. The head, knee and foot should all be in line before the hurdler extends the leg into the next stride.

The upper body

The upper body is bent slightly forward as the lead knee is being lifted to drive over the hurdle. That same body lean must be maintained into, over and away from the hurdle, the last action being the most important. This requires considerable abdominal strength, but pays tremendous dividends in maintaining momentum.

Where to take off

The athlete should be taking off in such a position that two-thirds of the distance covered is before the hurdle and one-third after: e.g. in the men's event, take-off should be about 2.4m before the hurdle and landing 1.2m after. Obviously the total distance is a little less when a lower hurdle is being cleared for the women's event and for younger athletes. If the before and after hurdle distances are close to even, e.g. 1.8m and 1.8m, then the hurdler is coming in too close and will be 'sailing' over the hurdle. This means that if the athlete comes in too near each hurdle, the take-off angle is up rather than out. Once launched into the air, there is

nothing that can be done to bring the athlete down any faster. It is common to see the unfortunate hurdler bend the knees, sink down a little, then launch themselves upwards over the hurdle. The resulting problem is that they must wait to return to the ground and when they do, they come down much harder than they would have done with an outward rather than upward push-off. The total time in the air is longer going up. The key to a better clearance is to develop the confidence and power to take off further away.

The high point of the clearance should be about 5cm before the hurdle. The athlete is literally stepping down over the hurdle.

Running between the hurdles

Hurdlers are sprinters and therefore it is essential to use the arms well between each hurdle. As in sprinting, the centre of gravity should be kept high. The athlete should be running off the toes and keeping the hips high.

Bend running

In the 400 metre hurdles half of the hurdles are on the bends. There is an advantage to leading with the left leg as the hurdler can stay on the inside of the lane. The rules of the event require hurdlers to stay within their lane – and this includes the air space! That means that the left-leg lead hurdler can run on the inside of the lane around the bends. The right-leg lead hurdlers must clear the hurdle towards the outer part of their lane to ensure that their trail foot does not come through in the next person's lane.

Another advantage for the left-leg lead hurdler is that the lean when clearing the hurdle is to the left, which means that there can be a continuation of the athlete's course around the bend. The right-leg lead hurdler briefly directs their momentum away from that curved run while clearing the barrier, and must therefore redirect their motion into the curve after landing.

Learning to hurdle from either leg

Because fatigue makes it difficult for the 400 metre hurdler to arrive at every barrier with the preferred lead leg, there is a great advantage in becoming proficient with take-off from either foot. It makes a great deal of sense to learn this skill as early as possible.

David Hemery on his way to a world record and Olympic gold in Mexico City, 1968

Former Commonwealth and European champion Alan Pascoe (UK, number 6)

TRAINING

Stamina

The conditioning programme should be aimed at fitness for 600 metres on the flat, as that distance equates best to the endurance demands of the 400 metre hurdles. Flat running fitness is important, but not sufficient by itself. Hurdling is physically very demanding; you are asking the body to run fast and put full effort into every clearance. With this in mind, it is important that sufficient hurdling is done to ensure there is hurdle endurance.

Strength to speed

Throughout the preparation of an athlete there has to be a progression whereby they move from endurance to speed as the emphasis. In all parts of the build-up there should be a mix of training. During the early training phase there should be some steady endurance running. Depending upon the athlete's age and capability, this could start say at a couple of miles and build up to 7–10 miles for adults. Even if the athlete is training throughout the year,

1986 Commonwealth champion Phil Beattie (Northern Ireland) ahead of Mark Holtom (England) at Gateshead

a couple of months will be a sufficient endurance mileage phase.

Most of the background speed endurance work should be over 500 metres–1,000 metres, obviously run at a speed which is greater than the steady distance pace. Three repetitions should be the norm. The recovery period is generally walking over the distance just run. The greatest emphasis should be in the 600 metre area. As the competitive season approaches – and during that season – I favour high quality runs with whatever recovery is necessary. e.g. 3×600 metres with 12–15 minutes rest between each.

Finishing a hurdling session with 1×600 metres is also a useful way of retaining over-distance track work.

Short recovery work is also important. This can be any distance from 40 metres to 400 metres. Two or three sets of 2×300 metres was a favourite of mine, the recovery on that session being a slow walk of the bend back to the start point. Recovery time for short distances repeats can be around thirty seconds, but having the pulse rate down below 120 beats per minute is the normal guide. The added advantage to doing this type of work is that it prepares the body and mind to continually pick up

Edwin Moses (USA), the double Olympic and world champion who has held the world record since 1976

the effort when feeling fatigued. That may sound rather a cruel type of training, but making the training for 400 metre hurdles harder than the racing is the key to running well in the event.

If you have sandhills nearby they are, in my view, the most valuable training commodity of all. If not, the next best training ground is hills. Training should never become too boring and hills can be a great asset; they vary in length and steepness so it is up to the athlete and coach to discover new and interesting locations.

Speed is a valuable asset which should not be neglected. If the athlete is prone to sprinting injuries, there is advantage in doing speed work over the hurdles.

Repetition hurdle sessions should be over at least five hurdles and occasionally the hurdler should run more than the total distance. e.g. 12 hurdles or 300 metres– 400 metres on the flat and then come over the last 5 hurdles. In the winter time, down and back hurdling over 50 m–80 m can be valuable repetition speed work.

Weight training, conditioning and

flexibility work should also be a part of every athlete's training throughout the year. Flexibility is vital to the hurdler for good clearance, but it will also help stride length and reduce the chances of injury.

There is no magic formula for training. Athletes who have reached the top over 400 metres by running longer distances and gradually reducing the volume and increasing the pace of training, have had success equal to those who have stayed with speed all along and done multiple repetitions. I tend to favour the former approach for 400 metre hurdles, as it has a strong endurance component; but it is all a matter of emphasis. The programme must incorporate something of everything. I prefer the gradual progression from quantity with less speed, to quality with greater speed. One rule of thumb which I have found helpful in reducing injuries and stress-induced sickness is to keep to a ratio of two hard days to one easy day, i.e. if someone is working out six days each week and work is hard on four of those days, the other two should be active recovery days.

Pace judgement

Once the weather allows you on to the track for spring hurdle training, it is best to practise 400 metre hurdles at the pace at which you want to race. By doing this, the stride pattern will be grooved in physically and mentally.

As in the flat 400 metres, there is a need to relax during a part of the race; usually that would be after establishing the initial speed and rhythm around the first bend. That pace can be maintained with less effort down the back straight, and the term 'floating' is sometimes used to describe that fast and loose motion which allows the athlete to run without straining – that is, relaxed.

SUMMARY

There is great benefit to be gained from the 400 metre hurdler learning to high-hurdle well. Aim in training to be fit enough to run well over 600 metres; hurdle frequently in training; use variety in the development of the programme and gradually change the emphasis from steady endurance running to speed and intensity. Training with intensity and over a long period of time is a key to improvement; however, it is also essential to have sufficient recovery days so as to stay enthusiastic and healthy. As a rule, if the intense sessions go beyond 66 per cent of the total, then the athletes are often running themselves down and thereby asking for injury or sickness. Athletics is to be enjoyed and hurdling can be one of the most interesting and enjoyable events. When one has reached the proficiency level of being able to flow over the hurdles and run powerfully between them, there is rarely a better feeling.

Part Three:
Jumping and Vaulting

GEOFF PARSONS

Geoff Parsons is the UK record-holder for the high jump

High Jump

In this section, I will try to outline those characteristics which I consider make for a sound high-jump technique.

To the young athlete, it is particularly important to jump in comfort, as today I know many top British jumpers who are prepared to jump in considerable pain, without actually studying their technique to find out what is causing it. I cannot make this point strongly enough: IF IT HURTS, DON'T DO IT.

While the basic ideas presented here will hold true for many high jumpers, it should always be remembered that every athlete is unique. My first coach had a saying which I believe to be one of the most sensible approaches to this sport: 'Every athlete is an experiment of one'. This means that the coach and the athlete should always be ready to try something different (although not necessarily new); but never to try it just for the sake of it. Every time a new world record holder appears, I see coaches forcing their athletes to copy the 'new' technique, often destroying much of what was already good in the athlete. When incorporating something new, try to do it within the framework of the athlete's existing technique.

Consider the present crop of world class high jumpers. Igor Paklin's technique will never be the same as Mogenburg's, which in turn will never be the same as that of Howard. All have jumped exceptionally high, but all are uniquely different and as far as they are concerned uniquely right. *Always remember that you are too.*

THE RUN UP

This section deals with the athlete's approach to the bar. Throughout I am using the Fosbury technique.

The first point to remember is that the run-up should be tailored to suit the athlete, not the athlete to the run-up. Its object is twofold:

1 To enable the athlete to arrive in the correct position and in the same place on every jump. Common sense thus suggests that we start at the same mark and use the same number of strides.

2 To enable the athlete to arrive at the take-off mark travelling at his or her optimum speed, i.e. as fast as he or she can control during the take-off phase.

Present-day coaches tend to favour a traditional D-turn approach, but I believe this has some fundamental problems. It encourages the athlete to plant his or her foot parallel to the bar, which is dangerously wrong because it tends to make the athlete travel along the bar rather than penetrating into the bed.

The following approach is one I would advocate for the young athlete. It is kinder on the ankle and knee joints, promotes a far better angle of foot plant, and gives the athlete far better penetration into the bed. I have not specified the number of strides required, as this is something for the individual athlete and coach to work out for themselves, although I would suggest 8–10 strides as being adequate to achieve your optimum jumping speed.

The run-up should be a unit, not two phases as is suggested in many texts. The athlete should be gradually accelerating from the very first stride, to the take-off point and through the jump phase. The curved nature of the run-up is to help the athlete lean away from the bar at take-off and into their centre of curvature.

THE JUMP PHASE

The jump phase is technically the most difficult stage to learn. It requires a far greater understanding of what we are trying to achieve than any other aspect of the jump.

It is a misconception that the athlete 'pushes' off the ground with their take-off leg. What gives you the height is the combination of speed, the pivotal action through the foot, and the elastic ability of your muscles to convert the generated momentum as quickly as possible from the horizontal to the vertical plane – in effect, a slingshot action.

It is essential that all the levers are used to their maximum during the jump phase. A dynamic and rangy inside leg is essential to a quality jump. Recent research suggests that as much as 40 per cent of your vertical energy is related to correct usage of the inside leg. The inside leg should be driven from behind the athlete, as fast as possible, and in a bent position. The knee should be driven in a straight line, *not*

Dick Fosbury startling the world with his 'flop' technique at the Mexico City Olympics in 1968. Since then, the Fosbury flop has been universally adopted

across the body, and should be held as high as possible for as long as possible.

Arm action at take-off is a subject of much debate at present. Personally speaking, I have always used a double arm shift, i.e. both arms behind the athlete at take-off; but recent research in Germany suggests that the single arm shift allows for a faster take-off. As speed of plant and take-off is the eventual limiting factor of every high-jumper, this technique is something I myself will be experimenting with in future years.

It is useful for the coach and athlete to analyse the jumper's position at the moment he or she leaves the ground. Ideally the athlete should be as tall and vertical as possible. The take-off leg should be fully extended at the knee and ankle.

Throughout the approach and jump phases, the athlete should try to 'think tall' at all times. The hips and mid-section particularly should be held high and tight, as any bending here leads to a loss of efficiency and propagates a sloppy jump.

Once the athlete has left the ground,

there is basically very little that can be done. Don't try to turn your back to the bar, because if all take-off procedures have been carried out correctly, the necessary rotaton will occur naturally.

Timing the layout is the major factor above the bar; this is something which will only develop with practice.

Don't form a violent arch over the bar. This is a bad habit which is noticeable at all levels of jumping. Only a very slight movement of the hips is required to clear it. Once the hips have cleared, the athlete should sit up towards the legs; this has the effect of pulling the legs away from the bar.

Rosie Ackermann (German Democratic Republic), former world record holder and last great exponent of the straddle technique
(Opposite) Sara Simeoni (Italy), former world record holder and 1980 Olympic champion

TRAINING

I stress that the views presented here are purely my own, related to my personal experience of what is required to achieve top class high-jumping. However, I will try to outline the basic areas the athlete should work towards.

There is no substitute for hard work when it comes to training. Even at an early age, the body will take reasonable quantities; but at all times the athlete should have the supervision of a good coach. Throughout the teenage years, the emphasis of training should be on all-round general conditioning. There are a surprising number of unfit high jumpers around. Not until the athlete has a good base of fitness should he or she progress to the more explosive and inherently more demanding jump work. The track, the multi-gym, grass and hill-running, the gymnasium and limited exposure to the heavy weights room – under strict super-

vision – should make up the bulk of the young athlete's work. The coach should try to make training interesting, and a challenge to the athlete's ability.

As the physique develops, training can be increased to include a greater proportion of plyometric (bounding and hopping) and hurdle jump/depth jump work, perhaps with trampolining and basic gymnastic skills being learned. Once this stage has been reached, it is then a matter of tailor-making the training for maximum potential.

Throughout the entire training life, I would suggest that there are two areas which should be particularly worked at. First, suppleness and mobility are absolutely essential assets of the modern high jumper; and second, coordination is important for both training and jumping, but is sadly overlooked in many training programmes.

Discipline is also important. There is discipline in actually going training and doing what is asked of you. The number of athletes I see who, when requested to do ten of an exercise, only do nine because 'the coach isn't looking', is quite unbelievable. The only person this hurts is yourself. A good coach has a sound reason for every piece of training, so if he says 'do ten' *then do them*! Remember, training you fail to do is training someone, somewhere else *is* doing – you can never catch up on that. In addition, the discipline of controlling your own body is very important.

Finally, I would add that the old adage of 'quality not quantity' is wrong in this context. To get to the top in British and world athletics requires quality *and* quantity.

SUMMARY

Competition preparation – both mental and physical – is something which can only be learnt from experience. A cool head, a mean streak and a never-say-die attitude are essential. Believe in your own ability and – although it might appear an unnecessary thing to say – *don't be afraid of winning!*

Even if your competitors are higher ranked than you on paper, remember that it is what happens on the day that counts, not what is written on the ranking lists.

The Indoor European Bronze Medal which I won in Madrid in 1986 was a medal gained by hanging in there and believing that I was as good as anyone competing, even though I was ranked only twelfth.

Finally, I would urge you to savour every achievement in training and competition – whether modest or momentous – and to fight through every problem; but above all and more important than anything I have said so far, have fun and enjoy high-jumping!

*Jimmy Howard (USA), a moment after take off. Note he is jumping **upwards***

MALCOLM SMITH, DIANA DAVIES' COACH, COMMENTS:

Diana's coordination promotes backwards rotation, leaving her in a good position for lay-out and regaining control of her free (left) leg

Flaws in Diana's technique have caused speed loss. The free knee has driven fast and straight, and the right thigh is parallel to the ground; but the right hip is thrown wide across the body instead of being raised up above the knee-level to reach the aimed-at height. The mid-section rotates too early, dropping the right shoulder, and the left arm now rises faster and higher than the right, causing the upper body to lean towards the bar.

  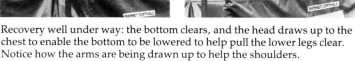

Safe landing

Recovery well under way: the bottom clears, and the head draws up to the chest to enable the bottom to be lowered to help pull the lower legs clear. Notice how the arms are being drawn up to help the shoulders.

(*Above*) Take-off preparation in its final phase: the leg, hip and trunk are kept in a straight line. The leg is pre-tensed ready for the plant, and its foot is pointing straight through the centre of the bar. The body is in line (*above right*), the hips are stabilizing to go through the plant, and the double arm shift is preparing the upper body

The run-up: the body must be in line, upright and leaning inwards of the curve, keeping the right shoulder higher than the left

The clearance. The body is well above the bar, and the head and shoulders are rising to promote the next phase.

Diana's gymnastic-strength ability is seen to good effect. The shoulders, having cleared the bar, are lowered to enable the hips to rise above the knees and form a natural arch.

Photographs such as these prove invaluable in training: Diana is a great British high jumper, and by analysing both technique faults and strengths, we work to improve the heights to 2 m-plus jumping

LYNN DAVIES

Lynn Davies was the 1964 Olympic long jump champion and still holds the UK record with a mark set in 1968

The Long Jump

The long jump appears a simple enough event when performed by a top athlete. Picture in your mind's eye the current women's world record holder, Heike Dreschler, in action. She accelerates down the runway, hits the board at great speed and climbs up and out across the sand, cycling her arms and legs to spray the sand over seven and a half metres away. She makes it look easy. The ease of performance, however, belies the many hours of training and practice required to excel at the long jump.

I was lucky to have been a natural athlete as a schoolboy, but it took a couple of hours' training every day, six days a week for over three years, to realize my full potential. Like all the field events in athletics, the long jump is a disciplined challenge. Speed on the runway must be controlled to ensure hitting the 8" take-off board, and converting the running speed into height at take-off must also be controlled and balanced to achieve good flight, landing and maximum distance. It is rare to get everything absolutely right. Something is usually lacking on each jump: slowing down at take-off, taking off behind the board, mistimed take-off and dropping the legs too soon on landing, are experiences common to all jumpers.

During my career, which spanned three Olympic Games and over twelve years of competition, there were only a couple of occasions when everything clicked and I felt I could not have improved on the distance. But the fun of field events is striving for that.

The main aspects of long jumping are approach runs; take-off; flight and landing. Think of Heike Dreschler again and the aim becomes clear – to blend together a fast controlled run up, powerful take-off, balanced flight and efficient leg start and landing.

APPROACH RUN

A fast accurate run up is the most important part of long-jumping. It is no good being a fast runner with great spring unless you can hit the board. Remember, competitions are won by a few centimetres. To establish a run up, I recommend the following method: use a lane on a running track, not a long-jump runway, and have a coach or partner assist you.

● Warm up thoroughly and do some fast strides over 50 metres so that you are moving well.

● Stand on a mark on the track and run over 40 metres. The first stride should be your jumping leg. Drive hard away from the mark and sprint naturally down the track.

● Recover fully between runs and repeat this 6–8 times. On each occasion your coach/partner will be noting where your 15th stride is landing and marking this on the track.

● Now measure the distance to where your furthest 15th stride landed with a tape measure and transfer this distance on to the long-jump runway, using the tape measure and marking back from the take-off board.

● Then try out the run up, remembering to begin the run with the jumping leg as your first stride. This should result in your take-off foot arriving near the board and will be your basic run up; it will be modified as you gain experience and can be increased to 17, 19 and 21 strides as you become stronger and faster.

● As you stand on the runway, it will give you great confidence to know that you are going to be close to the board with your take-off foot without having to chop and change your running strides.

TAKE-OFF AND FLIGHT

The aim at take-off is to drive up and out by planting the jumping foot down as quickly and firmly as possible and driving the knee and thigh of the other leg upwards in an exaggerated sprinting action. The hips and chest should be lifted off the board, then the leading leg extended and pulled back vigorously underneath the body. This will create a long, extended body shape in the air. The take-off leg now begins to come through and your arms will be circling forward overhead to help balance.

LANDING

As the landing approaches, bring both legs together as high as possible with the feet together. Your upper body will now be rotating forward and downward, but try to keep your feet and heels up for as long as possible. This will save vital inches.

When you hit the sand, give at the knees, keep your head low and think of pushing the hips forward and upward while your hands and arms are pulled through quickly to avoid falling back. All this happens in seconds, but will take hours of practice to master.

1964 Olympic champion, the incomparable Mary Rand of Great Britain. She was the first woman to jump over 22 feet, and she held the UK record for twenty-four years

TRAINING AND PRACTICE

Each of the aspects of long jump must be practised separately if you wish to improve, as well as working on the physical qualities necessary for top performance such as speed, strength and suppleness. It is qute a tough event on the ankles, knees, hips and back, and conditioning work is important to improve performance and avoid injury.

It is not necessary to have a coach with you for every training session; however, when you are beginning it really helps to have someone to make sure that you are doing things correctly and to watch the early stages of your progress.

It is also helpful to have someone to plan your training. The amount of time you spend training will depend on how keen you are to succeed. Remember that at the end of the day it is up to you.

Here are some guidelines to follow on training for long jump. Just as for track events, good field event athletes train all year round. In the winter it is important to build up strength and work on technique, so that when the competition season arrives you are in really good shape.

Work hard on your approach run until you can do it with your eyes closed. After a while, introduce a check mark five strides from the board which is your cue to accelerate into the take-off. Do 10–15 run-ups in a training session, not taking off but running through and hitting the board with your take-off foot. On the runway, think of a gradual acceleration from start to take-off.

Do lots of sprinting work, concentrating on good form. Run 6–12×150 metres per session in the winter, and flat out 50 metre sprints in the season. Also run the occasional 100 metre and relay race for the club if you are quick enough! Hurdling is a good event to practise as well.

Work on take-off by jumping off a short approach run of five strides, seven strides and nine strides. Think of a good range of movement at take-off. *Think about what you are doing.* It helps to work off a gymnasium box top or bent board occasionally, to give you height and time to work in the air. Try to work with a coach when doing this.

Build up your leg power with plenty of leg conditioning drills. Start by hopping on one leg over 30 metres, then build up to 100 metres. Giant bounding is excellent. Weight training is a must, but work under supervision. Circuit training is good too and ensures that all the major muscle groups are strengthened.

Finally, try to learn as much as you can about the event by reading and by discussing it with other athletes. Watch top long-jumpers whenever you can and analyse them. Create a picture in your mind of the kind of jumper you wish to be.

Good luck in your athletics. I hope you have as much fun, enjoyment and satisfaction from your long-jumping as I did.

A TYPICAL WEEK OF TRAINING

MONDAY
Warm up. 6 practice run ups (without take-off). 8–12 jumps from seven strides. 4–6×150 metres.

TUESDAY
Warm up. 6×60 metres, 6×30 metres hopping; 3×each leg. 3×150 metres.

WEDNESDAY
Warm up. 3 run ups (without take-off). 3 full out jumps. 4–6×150 metres. 3–6×4 flights of hurdles.

THURSDAY
Warm up. 6×60 metres. 3 run ups. 6 jumps from seven to nine strides.

FRIDAY
Rest or easy jogging. Striding and stretching. 30–40 mins.

SATURDAY
Competition.

SUNDAY
Rest.

Heike Dreschler (German Democratic Republic), world record holder and world champion

LYNN DAVIES COMMENTS:

Kim Hagger
demonstrates a 1½ hitch
kick technique

The run-up. Kim maintains her speed over the last five strides, running tall and looking straight ahead. The plant is firm.

The opposite thigh and knee are driven up as in a vigorous sprint action. The arms make an exaggerated sprint action to assist take-off

The take-off leg now flexes and extends. Body is upright, and arms are held overhead.

The other leg comes through and extends alongside the leading leg. Body and legs rotate forwards and downwards. Legs are kept as high as possible, and arms are extended and parallel with the legs.

The hips and chest move upwards and forwards: the non-take-off leg now moves downwards and underneath the body. Notice that Kim's arms circle to maintain a good balance in the air

Kim shows control in mid-air, with an effective range of arm and leg movements leading to an excellent leg shoot at the end to gain maximum distance. From take-off to landing is less than two seconds. Technique develops each element of the jump, which are then blended into one smooth continuous movement

Heels break the sand ahead of the hips. Knees flex, and arms move forwards and upwards to take body weight over the feet. Some jumpers like to fall sideways and put one hand out for support

ANDY ASHURST

Andy Ashurst won the 1986 Commonwealth Games pole vault

Pole Vault

Pole-vaulting requires an all-round ability, combining the speed and strength of a sprinter/long-jumper with the agility and nerve of a gymnast. My advice to anyone taking up this event is to get the basics drilled in right from the start and to ensure that training is specific to the requirements of pole-vaulting, paying equal attention to the major muscle groups involved (i.e. legs, abdominal/dorsal, shoulders/arms). Once good technique has been learned, gains in speed and strength alone should lead to improvements in performance. It is very hard to be successful with poor technique even if one is extremely talented physically; and furthermore, bad habits are very hard to change.

I was lucky to be properly taught the basics at an early age (12 years old). This has enabled me to be successful despite being poorly gifted in both leg speed and power. I was introduced to vaulting by pure fluke when the club was short of someone for a young athletes' club meeting – I volunteered and won the event with a vault of 2.00m! More youngsters should be given the chance to 'have a go'. With the correct guidance and training, pole-vaulting over a high bar is a thrilling experience.

The vault itself can be divided into three sections, each requiring their own specific training methods. They are the approach run, the plant/take off phase, and the swing up/push off phase.

THE APPROACH RUN

The approach run is becoming increasingly critical as vaulters' grips get higher and higher. The speed of the run determines to a large extent the height at which one can grip a pole, which in turn determines the height to be achieved, given a sound vaulting technique.

It is important to run 'tall', with high knees and full extension of the rear leg, and to accelerate gradually into the plant and take-off. This running style must be drilled into the early stages of learning, even when using low grips and short approach vaults. The length of the run-up will vary considerably among vaulters. But whatever stride pattern is chosen, the vaulter should always be aiming for maximum controllable speed at take-off. It is also very important to run 'relaxed' and to keep the pole stable in order to perform a smooth transition from the approach run into the plant and take-off.

Training

Of the training time devoted to sprinting and running drills, I would recommend that at least 50 per cent of this is performed carrying a pole, because it is such a specific skill. There are a vast number of training routines which will help to develop sprinting speed and power. I will concentrate on exercises specifically related to the approach run in the vault.

1 Acceleration runs over 30–50 m with a pole, concentrating on correct running style.

2 Sprint drills over 20–30 m with a pole, such as 'high knees', 'heel flicks', 'reach and claw'.

3 Hopping and bounding with a pole over a short distance, trying to keep the body in an upright and controlled position. (*Note:* These should be done with a small, light pole to start with.)

4 Running with a pole over 8–10 low hurdles (30cms) or sticks placed on the ground at certain intervals (1–2 metres apart), making sure the vaulter does not look down at the ground.

(*Note:* To make these exercises more beneficial, it is better to use poles which are slightly longer and heavier than normal.)

THE PLANT AND TAKE-OFF

This is the most important part of the vault to get right. If you are off balance or in the wrong position here, the rest of the vault becomes progressively harder to control. It is the area where many common mistakes can be seen, particularly among beginners who have not received adequate training in the basic techniques. In order to perfect this phase it is necessary to repeat the action many times, concentrating on the skills that make a good plant and take-off.

The vaulter must maintain the speed produced on the run-up and remain tall over the last few strides of the approach run. The pole should be planted into the box early with the top arm stretched high above the head and the take-off foot directly below the top hand. The vaulter must concentrate on stretching the body as tall as possible and jumping at take-off (as in the long-jump). The pole vault take-off must be made active. As the vaulter leaves the ground, he must keep the top arm straight and drive up into the pole leading with the chest, but not allowing the hips to swing forward too quickly. The direction of drive of the non-take-off leg should be made vigorously in a forward/upward direction. As the vaulter moves forward and the pole bends, the rear leg driving off the ground should remain straight for a short while. The position of the head at this stage varies, but as long as it is looking upwards and not down at the box the vaulter need not worry too much.

Training

The best way to perfect this action is to do

Keith Stocke (UK), Commonwealth record holder

Brian Hooper bends the pole. He broke the British record seventeen times, equalling Geoff Capes' number of shot records

pop-ups. These are done off a 6–8-stride approach, with a low grip so that the pole does not bend. It is a very simple exercise and can be performed many times in a training session, but it is important to concentrate on doing it correctly and not just go through the motions. The vaulter must stay 'tall' and jump off the ground.

Here are the important exercises:
1 Running along the track, planting the pole several times.
2 Planting on grass and swinging through (very low grips!)

3 Planting on to a towel or sliding box placed on the track.
4 Planting into a sand-pit and swinging through.
Other exercises include:
1 Running on to a swinging rope and driving off the ground.
2 Short-approach long-jumping, emphasizing the active take-off.
3 Jumping exercises over low hurdles, driving high with the leading knee and keeping the back leg as straight as possible for as long as possible.

THE SWING-UP/PUSH-OFF PHASE

After the take-off, it is important to keep driving with the leading knee and to keep the arms and chest active. It is a common mistake to hang on to the pole and expect it to recoil and throw the vaulter over the bar – this simply does not happen. The vaulter must work every bit of the way up to and over the bar, and can only relax once he is clear and on the way down to the landing area.

It is essential to drive the pole forward towards the pit with the chest, arms and legs, then to rock-back using the arms and abdominal/thigh flexor muscles. The back arm (right arm for a right-handed vaulter) must drive, but must be kept straight until the vaulter has inverted with hips up and shoulders back. Then as the pole straightens, he must use both arms to heave the rest of the body up towards the bar, keeping the line of the body as close to the line of the pole as possible. The head should be kept in line with the rest of the body, so as the vaulter extends towards the bar the head should be looking down at the bottom hand (left hand). The pull up towards the bar should be maintained for as long as possible as the vaulter performs a half twist before reaching the bar. As the vaulter's legs and hips are clearing the bar, the vaulter must push off the pole. When the vaulter has let go of the pole, he must not throw the head and arms back to clear the bar because this often makes the chest drop on to the bar and knock it off. I have fallen into this trap many times and have learnt to avoid it by curling my arms under and around the bar and relaxing while performing this action. The higher one jumps

and the more effective the push-off, the more time one gets to finish this part of the vault successfully.

Training

Training for this part of the vault consists almost entirely of gymnastic type exercises, because once the vaulter has left the ground he becomes a gymnast.

ROPE WORK
1   Rope swings – catching hold of a swinging rope, driving forward, swinging up and rocking back (one leg either side of the rope).
2   Rock-back and extend on a stationary rope.
3   Rope climbs using:
(a) arms and legs.
(b) arms only.
(c) upside down (gripping rope with feet above the hands).
(d) upside down using two adjacent ropes.

RINGS
1   Muscle ups.
2   Rock-back and extend.
3   Any other relevant exercises.

HIGH BAR
1   Chin-ups using vault grip/undergrasp/over grasp.
2   Muscle ups and upstarts.
3   Upward circles.
4   Tucking knees up to chest while hanging with arms fully extended.

The grim determination of Keith Stocke is shown clearly here

WALL BARS
1 Rock-backs hanging with arms fully extended, touching the wall above the hands.
2 Leg circles.

FLOOR WORK
1 Handstands.
2 Walking on hands.

3 Backward roll to handstand.
4 Handstand press-ups (partner holding the legs).

OTHER TRAINING
Back stretching exercises and mobility are necessary to complete the conditioning part of the training.

SUMMARY

The only aspect of pole-vaulting not mentioned so far is the mental training. Once the element of fear has been overcome, then there is no reason why learning the basics correctly and doing the relevant conditioning should not result in being a successful pole-vaulter.

JEFF GUTTERIDGE, THE TOP BRITISH INTERNATIONAL POLE

The penultimate stride before take-off. The pole is lifted in preparation for the high, overhead plant

As the right foot strikes the ground, the left hand pushes the pole towards the back of the box

The end of the final stride: the pole is lifted high above the head

The rock-back phase, with the left leg beginning to flex

The legs lift into the tuck position

A tight tuck is achieved before the pole straightens

Hips now above the top hand; Jeff pushes with that hand

Release of the pole. Note the straight right arm, indicating a forceful push off the pole

VAULTER, IN TRAINING

Just before take-off – note the straight left arm which will assist the bending of the pole

(*Above*) Take-off: both arms are straight and, with the chest, they press the pole up and forwards. The hang phase (*above right*), continues to drive body forward and maintains an upright position to effect maximum bending of the pole. The flexed right knee creates forward momentum. The fully extended take-off leg indicates a powerful jump

The beginning of the extension stage. With his back parallel to the ground, Jeff now pushes vigorously upwards from his hips

Extension almost complete: Jeff pulls strongly along the line of the pole to lift the hips towards the top hand

The vault almost complete – Jeff lifts arms and chest upwards and backwards to clear the bar

JOHN HERBERT

John Herbert (left) won the 1986 Commonwealth Games triple jump and is a former winner of the European Cup triple jump

The Triple Jump

The technique of the triple jump appears simple, but it is much more than a variation of the long jump. The athlete has an approach run, hops from one foot and lands on the same foot, steps on to the other foot, pulls the leg through and lands on both feet simultaneously. Performance is a composite, a total of three separate efforts. The triple jumper must be a versatile athlete possessing jumping strength, jumping agility, endurance and also spring.

Zdislaw Hoffmann (Poland), 1983 world champion

APPROACH RUN

The task of an approach run is to produce a high (optimum) horizontal velocity and to prepare for an effective take-off from the board. The approach is sub-divided into two sections: the acceleration, in which two-thirds of the distance is covered; and the preparatory rhythm, involving the last 5–6 strides' surge, on to and past the board. A jumper's approach run varies between 34 and 45 metres, involving an average of 18–24 strides. Jumpers with good acceleration will naturally require a shorter approach than those who must run a longer distance to achieve the necessary speed to jump. Almost every jumper has his own method of beginning his approach. Some jumpers use a standing start, others a few strides before their approach, trying to reach maximum speed quickly.

The most important thing is that the beginning stays the same for each run-up, so the jumper becomes precise in hitting the board. The start of the run-up for each jumper must have a relatively high speed, where the acceleration forward is smooth and relaxed for as long as possible. This acceleration should take you to the second section of the run-up, the last 5–6 strides in which the preparation for the first take-off takes place. During the last few strides, there should be a transition from acceleration to a higher pace, where stride length is reduced. This causes the jumper's centre of gravity to be much higher for the first take-off at the board. You must think 'running tall'.

THE HOP

Like all other jumps, the hop consists of a take-off, flight phase and landing. The take-off must be executed rapidly. Whichever leg you take off from after the approach run, is the leg you land on. The body's centre of gravity must be high. The extension of the leg at take-off is assisted by the swinging of the free leg and arms. The free leg is swung in a horizontal position like a short pendulum; the swinging movement of the arm is adapted to the running rhythm; the upper body should be erect and the counteracting movement of the arms maintains balance.

During the flight, the jumper performs the reversing of the legs which corresponds to the first part of the flight phase. By reversing the leg, the athlete prepares for an effective landing and the subsequent take-off for the step. The thigh of the take-off leg should be lifted from the hip as high as possible, waiting for the ground where a reaching position comes naturally from which a landing can take place, a striking movement down and back 'pawing'. This keeps the braking and rotating impulses as low as possible.

THE STEP

The specifications outlined for the hop are basically the same for the step; this is the shortest of the three jumps and takes place under difficult conditions. Once the hop has occurred, there must be a swinging movement 'up and out' of the free leg from the hip into a horizontal position. The better the stretching and swinging movement, the more effective the take-off will be. Keep upper body erect. The movement of the arms is synchronized with the leg to maintain balance. The thigh of the swinging leg is held in advance by a reaching movement forward and upward and then brought down for the active landing.

World record holder Willie Banks (USA)

THE JUMP

After the step, it is best for the jumper to think of the last phase as a long jump, the only difference being the horizontal speed. The jumper will not be able to bring his legs as far to the front as in the long jump.

Following the landing of the step, the free leg is swung upward and held for as long as possible in the horizontal position; the body should be kept erect, arm high to keep the centre of gravity high and to stop forward rotation in the flight curve. The jumper must try to lift his legs. The hips are shifted forward above the flight curve, and the jumper will assume 'the sitting position' for landing. Just before landing the arms are carried high, where the body will be swung vigorously forward when the heels have broken the sand.

TRAINING

Training for the triple jump is a combination of weight training, running, box work, bounding flexibility and technical training. All of these aspects, of course, have different loadings in terms of the athlete's age and standard. This is an example of the year plan of an international jumper:

NOVEMBER–JANUARY
All-round weight training, running, bounding, (60 m–100 m).

FEBRUARY–MARCH
Increase weight training, bounding (100 m–150 m). Some specialized work.

APRIL–MAY (Competition begins in May)
Fast running, actual triple jumping from short approach, speed bounding 20 m–40 m.

MAY–SEPTEMBER
Competitions throughout the season, first sprints 20 m, 30 m, 40 m, 50 m, 60 m, triple tech from short approach, speed bounding 20 m–40 m.

The following is an example of a 6-week cycle for an international jumper.

WEEK 1

SUNDAY
Hurdle drills
Sprint drills
(150×5)×3
Depth jumps (specific)
Technique – walk, jog on
General overall conditioning

MONDAY
Light weight training/depth
Verticals
Hurdle drills (jumps)
Back to back 100 m (2×10)
Speed/sprint circuit
General overall conditioning

TUESDAY
Hurdle drills
Depth jumps
(300 m×5)×2
Hurdle drills (jumps) and long-jump take-offs
General overall conditioning and med ball

WEDNESDAY
Weight training 80%
Bounding to 150 hops
Speed/sprint circuit and blocks technique

THURSDAY
Hurdle drills
Sprint drills
(200×4)×3
Long-jump drills and take-offs
Technique work and jog-ons
General overall conditioning

FRIDAY
Rest day

SATURDAY
Hills over 100 m – 2×5
Bounding to 100 hops/steps
Speed/sprint circuit

WEEK 2

SUNDAY
(150×5)×3

MONDAY
Light weight training
Bounding to 150 steps
Sprint circuit

TUESDAY
Hurdle drills
(300 m×5)×2

WEDNESDAY
Weight training 80%

Bounding to 150 hops/steps
Speed/sprint circuit and blocks technique

THURSDAY
(200×10)×2

FRIDAY
Rest day

SATURDAY
Hills over 100 m – 2×5
Bounding up hills to 40 m
(bunnies, hops/steps)
Speed/sprint circuit

WEEK 3

SUNDAY
(150×6)×3

MONDAY
Same as week 1

TUESDAY
Hurdle drills
Depth jumps
(250×6)×2

WEDNESDAY
Weight training 80%
Bounding to 150 hops

THURSDAY
(200×10)×2

FRIDAY
Rest day

SATURDAY
As for week 1

WEEK 4

SUNDAY
(150×6)×3

MONDAY
Same as week 2

TUESDAY
(400/300/250)×3

WEDNESDAY
Weight training 80%

Bounding to 150 hops/steps

THURSDAY
(200×5)×3

FRIDAY
Rest day

SATURDAY
As for week 2

WEEK 5

SUNDAY
Hurdle drills
Sprint drills
(180/170/160 etc. down to 90)
80 (walk back recovery)
5–9 strides technique

MONDAY
Light weight training/depth
Verticals
Hurdle drills (jumps)
Back to back 100 m
(2×8)

TUESDAY
Hurdle drills
(300×3)×2
Speed/sprint
circuit and blocks technique
Short runs

WEDNESDAY
Rest day

THURSDAY
Sprint drills
(200×5)×2
Technique
5–9 strides
General overall conditioning

FRIDAY
Rest day

SATURDAY
Hills over 100 m– 2×5
Speed sprint circuit and blocks short runs

WEEK 6

SUNDAY
$(300\times4)\times2$

MONDAY
Rest day

TUESDAY
$4\times500\,m$

WEDNESDAY
Rest day

THURSDAY
$(150\times4)\times3$

FRIDAY
Rest day

SATURDAY
Rest day

Recovery

500 m – 5 mins
400 m – 3 mins
300 m – 2 mins
250 m – 1½ mins
200 m – 1 min
150 m – 45 secs
100 m – 30 secs

Between sets

6 mins (400/300/250)
5 mins
4 mins
3 mins
2 mins
5 mins

JOHN HERBERT TRAINING INDOORS AT HARINGEY

The first phase, the hop: double arm-shift at take-off

Excellent take-off leg extension and high knee pick-up: the take-off leg comes through flexed and forward for landing

Into the take-off for the second phase, the step. Note the double arm shift

A hitch-kick into the pit

A wide range of movement helps gain maximum distance on this first phase. Arms are moving backwards ready for the second take-off

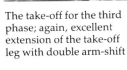

The rear leg is held high as it comes through for landing

The take-off for the third phase; again, excellent extension of the take-off leg with double arm-shift

Landing: John will pivot over his feet by swinging his arms forward

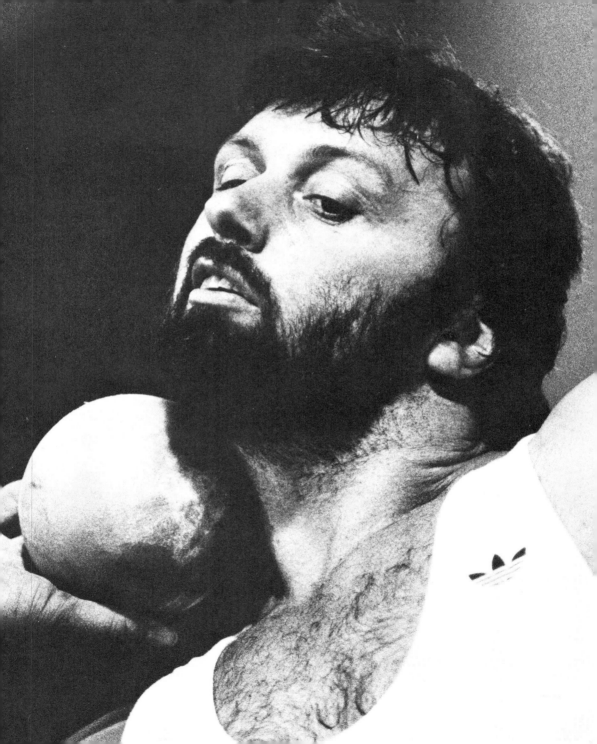

Part Four: Throwing

GEOFF CAPES

Geoff Capes has held the UK record for shot put for fifteen years, and has twice won the Commonwealth title

Shot Put

Good shot putting requires a basic '5S' programme:
1 Strength
2 Stamina
3 Suppleness
4 Speed
5 Skill

It also requires aggression, and for those aspiring to reach the very top, height is a major consideration; very few world-class putters are under 6' 3". Early in their careers shot putters should look to be good all-round athletes. I was lucky enough to have these attributes – I was very fast over sixty metres: I could run a presentable 400 metres and I could hurdle and jump. Coaches and athletes must look well into the future, to the time when the athlete must be putting the 9.26k shot. This is probably where we have lost our way in recent years by concentrating coaching efforts on the small aggressive type of putter who, when he has reached the senior standard, has found the task of propelling the shot to international distances beyond his capability. Young shot putters who are not gaining success at schools level may take comfort from the fact that I finished 22nd in the schools event in 1964!

THE 5S PROGRAMME

Strength

The strength required is immense – nobody can project a missile a long way unless they are strong. In the strength programme, when you start lifting, how you start lifting and what sort of programme you follow are all vitally important.

Stamina

In a major championship (and I include schools), you have six throws each; but each of those six throws may only come round once every twenty minutes. It requires great overall concentration, but you also have to concentrate even more and create energy for one split second every twenty minutes. This can only be accomplished successfully if you have included stamina work in your training programme.

Suppleness

You have to get into near-contortionist positions in order to attain the range of movement necessary to project the missile over a great distance. However, you can only apply this movement within the confines of the circle – in the shot, a seven-foot circle. If the circle had a greater radius, then I think we would throw further! If you cannot fully achieve the body position required by the technique then you will not be able to attain the range of movement to create the speed to project the missile. It is as simple as that. The aspiring shot putter, therefore, *must* be supple.

Speed

You need to be explosive because of the restriction of the circle; it is necessary to accelerate and release within the circle within a split second, and thus generate an enormous amount of 'explosion'. Work must be undertaken, therefore, to educate the body over a short period of time. I did a great deal of hurdling and high jumping in my career – events one would not normally expect to see a shot putter undertaking because of his size, but they were included to train one to attain a controlled application of speed.

Skill

Skill is individual within your technique. There are a variety of techniques, though by far the most popular is the O'Brien style, named after the great American shot putter of the fifties, Parry O'Brien. Whatever the technique, though, you have to apply it to the individual concerned. Throwers must capitalize on their abilities, so it is important to find out strengths and weaknesses and vary technique accordingly.

FUNDAMENTALS OF TECHNIQUE

The O'Brien Technique

When O'Brien developed his technique back in the fifties, he found that by facing the back of the circle rather than the side in the classic 'porridge oats' position of hitherto, he could apply force to the shot over a greater distance. This is basically what the shot putter is trying to do – apply maximum force over a maximum distance. The technique is fairly simple. For a right-handed thrower:

1 Place your right foot on the rear of the circle in the eleven to twelve o'clock position with the left foot lightly touching the circle.
2 Then adopt a basic 'T' position with a slight right-leg bend. The shot is rested in the neck with left arm relaxed, pointing backward.
3 'Push' or 'drive' across the circle at great speed, with the right foot landing in the centre. Momentarily afterwards, the left foot lands at the stop board between five and six o'clock. The weight is over the bent right leg. The athlete should have a pattern to think of such as right foot – right foot – left foot. In my mind I think of one – one – two or a – b – c. Sometimes, you can actually hear the feet landing; it is a recoil 'cocking' action.
4 The right foot moves into a running position ready to instigate the drive at the front of the circle. The left foot must not come into a block position, but must be above five o'clock at the front of the circle.
5 The right foot drive commences to drive and lift the shot: the action is foot-knee-hip-drive. Eyes should be projected still to the far distance (for me, 100 metres

away). Keep looking back as long as is practical and remembering that once you move your head, everything else moves forward as well. The drive begins. The object, of course, is to bring into play initially the larger and stronger muscle groups.
6 Keep yourself relaxed throughout the movement. You are an elastic band, not a broomstick! It is a recoil action that is required in shot putting and not a rigid action.
7 Keep the shoulders back as long as possible, so that you are in a 'torque' position.
8 The left and right foot remain on the ground for as long as possible. Once either foot leaves the ground, then the putt is over because you cannot apply force from or against thin air.
9 The hip lifts against the braced but relaxed left leg. As the shot passes over the left leg, the arm comes into play and the legs reverse.

Shorter throwers (under 6'3" in height) have to compensate at the back of the circle. There is an over-rotation of the shoulders, an exaggeration of the torque, with the left arm slightly more bent and over-rotated by a dipped left shoulder. In theory this gives a greater range of movement to enable you to catch up on your taller counterpart.

Important points to remember

1 Learn the basic rudiments of throwing.
2 Don't learn a formalized technique too

young, because as you get older you become taller and stronger and hopefully more supple. Between 15 and 19 years of age, dramatic changes in your body take place. So learning fundamental basics is important, but don't be stereotyped.

3 Don't over-complicate the technique too early.

4 Make the event itself as attractive as possible by, for instance, introducing games with the shot, e.g. overhead throwing, through-the-leg throwing, left-handed throwing for a right-handed thrower and vice-versa. This will also help to educate the other parts of the body which, if you just stick with the rigid technqiue of throwing, would not be developed.

(Right) Udo Beier (German Democratic Republic) beginning his glide. The whole emphasis of his stance is to the rear of the circle. He will not commence to 'unwind' until his left foot hits the ground

TRAINING

Strength

Weight Training
Train the most powerful muscle groups – legs, arms, back. Concentrate on the main weight-lifting events:

(a) bench press
(b) squat
(c) dead lift

Variations:
(d) frontal squat
(e) three-quarter squat
(f) step-ups
(g) sit-ups
(h) power clean
(i) power snatch
(j) bench press – vary the grip

Weight train every day and, when possible, even during the competitive season. There is no substitute for strength in a throwing event. Go to a proper gymnasium and have a proper coach. Don't be self-taught. Bad weight training habits can stay with you for life.

Suppleness

I had a hurdles coach for a shot coach, and so I went through a whole programme of suppling work!
1   Hurdling
2   Hurdling exercises
3   General stretching in a warm-up sense
I would go through a whole programme of suppleness exercises before lifting and I recommend every putter – in fact, every athlete – to do so. I would go so far as to say that because of their size, shot putters need more, not less, suppleness and stretching work than an ordinary athlete prior to every session.

Skill

Find a coach very early on to help you tap your talent. With our coaching infrastructure, a club coach can put you on the right track – you need that coaching eye.

In the early days, half of the training time should be devoted to technique. As the athlete becomes more and more proficient, so less time can be spent here. I think that generally in Britain we spend far too much time developing technique and not enough on the other ingredients required to make a champion athlete.

Speed

$Mass \times Force \times Speed = Distance$. All the exercises you see a sprinter doing – do them and more! If necessary, go to a sprint coach and get his advice.
1   Sprinting – 20–40 metres
2   Vertical jumps
3   Shuttle runs
4   Standing jumps (long and triple)
5   Bounding exercises
Again, do this work throughout the year.

Stamina

Fartlek and cross-country. Try to run 2 miles every other training session. Run before other forms of training, such as weight training and technique work. The furthest I ever ran was 20 miles, but this is not strictly necessary!

SUMMING UP

As far as throwing is concerned, aim to build on the basic animal requirements.

BILLY COLE IN TRAINING

Remaining relaxed, Billy drops and extends his shoulders as far out at the back of the circle as possible, arriving in the classic 'T' position.

A good 'power position'. The hips are set side-on to the shoulders to give a good body torque, the right foot has turned through almost 90°, and Billy comes up on his toe, allowing him to turn his leg and hip to the front ahead of his arm.

The right leg and hip turn and extend, rotating the trunk to the front. The left leg and side of the body brace strongly to accelerate the right side of the body. The legs complete their extension, and the elbow is kept high and behind the shot to facilitate maximum transition of force into the shot.

The glide phase brings the thrower into a firm position for launching the shot. The athlete must stay loose and low: you cannot apply your 'power' too early. The left leg reaches for the stopboard, and the right leg drives.

Billy keeps his eye on the shot for as long as possible, to ensure that his whole goes into the direction of the throw, 'chasing the shot out'. Above left shows excellent extension over the board: above right demonstrates how comfortable the recovery is.

Force must be applied to the shot over the greatest range in the shortest time and as near as possible in a straight line. The path of acceleration must therefore be long, and the transition from the back to the front of the circle smooth to ensure the least loss of momentum and maximum velocity at release.

GRAHAM SAVORY

Graham Savory was the 1986 UK champion in the discus

Discus

In this section I hope to pass on some of my international experience on technique, training through the year and preparing for competition.

THE DISCUS TECHNIQUE

My own technique is broken down into four different stages, which need to be joined into the whole throw by rhythm and flow.

Meg Ritchie, Commonwealth champion 1982 and UK record holder since 1976

The wind up

The most important point at this stage is to be long, slow and relaxed. The arm should be long and level with the shoulders, feet shoulder-width apart at the back with most weight leaning on the left leg. Start the wind up slowly, enabling you to reach the next stage with ease and in a good position. Going too fast from the back will shorten your arm and loosen your position, making you fall into the centre of the circle unbalanced.

The balance

Body weight is used to effect speed and position into the middle of the circle. From the wind up, move your weight over the left knee at the back of the circle. This moves your body's centre of gravity down a line which runs through your left shoulder, left knee and foot.

With most of the body weight over the left leg, this allows the right leg to be swept out and around. The left side of the body works as a pivot. The thrower is balanced and the weight moves to the middle of the circle. From this point the body weight must be channelled straight across the circle; look and drive along the right-hand sector line. By keeping your eyes fixed along the sector line, the left leg drives the feet quickly underneath the body and keeps the upper body slower. This gives you a long pull on the discus.

The power position

This position is where both feet have landed – the right foot on or across the centre line towards the front half of the circle and the left foot at the front of the circle. The left toe should be in line with the right heel. The upper body is leaning over the right leg, with the right arm held at 90 degrees to the upper body (the high point).

The body lean gives better height at the delivery. The height of the right arm is very important, for if it is at 90 degrees you can use gravity to pull down on the discus and accelerate its speed into delivery (it works just like a 'Big Dipper' at the fair). Once the arm reaches the high point, the discus will follow its own plane.

Always try to keep the arm at 90 degrees to the body during the whole throw. This will give you the maximum range with the discus. If the arm is not kept at this level it shortens the range, reducing the distance.

The block

The block has the effect of stopping the body movement and allowing the power to be passed into the discus. The only way I can explain this to you is to suggest you imagine that the left side of your body stops dead, like hitting a wall.

When the left side is blocked, the right foot can turn and by turning the right foot out it will force the right hip against the left hip. This makes the thrower extend on to the toes of his left foot and the whole body will lift into the delivery at the front of the circle. The most important part of the block, apart from locking the left side, is to keep the right foot turning. The block together with the plane of the discus will give maximum speed and height at the delivery.

After the release of the discus the technique becomes totally personal so long as you stay within the confines of the circle. Some throwers keep their feet down, while most throwers have an active reverse due to their feet leaving the ground at delivery.

I feel I differ from many throwers in the way I join the throw together. The best way to understand the rhythm is to watch a good discus thrower; try to get a film or video of the thrower and play it through many times. Build up a mental picture of the throw, its speed and rhythm. You will find that after some time the speed and rhythm will fall into place with your technique.

TRAINING

Training is dependent on the ability and age of the athlete. Being a senior international, I train seven days a week, but this has been gradually built up since I started in the event at the age of seventeen. Training should increase slowly over the years; I have seen many youngsters train too hard too soon and because of this have become disillusioned with the sport.

Below are details of my own training, which is for a high level of competition. Do not try to copy this schedule, but select parts of it that can be applied to yourself.

Year plan

I use periodization for my year's training. This enables me to peak at least twice a year, once in the winter and once in the summer. If there are two major competitions during the summer, I aim for two peaks.

OCTOBER–NOVEMBER

Conditioning – running, fitness work and mobility.
Weight training – low weights, high repetitions.
Throwing – technique drills working on major faults from the summer.

NOVEMBER–FEBRUARY

Strength phase: weight training – heavy weights, low repetitions.
Throwing – long sessions working to transfer drills into full throw.
Running – sprints up to 60 metres, sand jumping and mobility.

FEBRUARY–MARCH

For me this includes an indoor shot season, bringing in my winter peak.
Throwing – high quality, shorter competitive sessions.
Weight training – major lifts 85%, Olympic lifts to maximum
Running – sprints; short, sharp maximum 30 metres.

MARCH–MAY

Strength phase – as November–February, but at a higher level due to strength gained earlier. Throwing distances should have increased.

MAY–SEPTEMBER

Competitive season: throwing – high quality, shorter sessions.
Weight training – major lifts 85%, Olympic lifts to maximum.
Running – short sprints and sand jumping.
Below is a typical week's training schedule during winter and summer.

WINTER

MONDAY
Weights – bench press, full squats, dead lift.
3 specific lifts for discus i.e. flat flies, lat pull downs and curls.
2 abdominal exercises.

TUESDAY
15 minutes warm-up and mobility. Throwing – technique session up to 50 throws.
Sprints and jumps.

WEDNESDAY
Weights – cleans, front squat, clean pulls.
3 specific lifts – wide bench inclined flies, tricep push down.
2 abdominal exercises.

THURSDAY
As Tuesday.

FRIDAY
Weights – snatch, inclined bench, behind neck press (lifts to assist shot put).
3 specific lifts.
2 abdominals.

SATURDAY
Warm up etc.
Throwing – Long technical session, 50 throws plus shot put technique.
Step runs.

SUNDAY
As Saturday

Weights

Major lifts – *Week one* 8 sets of 5 reps to maximum for 5.
Week two 8 sets of 3 to max. Specific lifts, 6 sets of 6. Abdominals, 4 sets of 20.

SUMMER

MONDAY
Weights – bench press, toe squats, high pulls.
3 specific lifts.
2 abdominal exercises.

TUESDAY
Warm up etc.
Throwing – 3 sets of 6 throws high quality, competitive.
Sprints and jumps.

WEDNESDAY
Weights – cleans, snatch, front squats.
3 specific lifts.
2 abdominal exercises.

THURSDAY
Warm up etc.
Throwing – 2 sets of 6 throws with light-weight discus, working for speed.
Sprints.

FRIDAY
Rest day before competition.

SATURDAY
Competition.

SUNDAY
Post mortem on competition the day before; technique session.

Weights

Major lifts – 85% of best weight for 5 reps, 6 sets of 5.
Specific lifts, 4 sets of 10.
Abdominals, 4 sets of 20.

SUMMARY

There are a number of points to remember. Never foul your throw in training to throw further: remember, the circle is only 8ft 2ins. Always feel that you have learnt something positive from every session and set yourself attainable targets. It is always better to finish your session having reached your target, rather than getting upset at not breaking the world record!

In competition never warm up too hard; in this way too many people waste their best throw. The six competition throws are where the medals are won. Keep to the warm-up used in training. Always be prepared for any conditions; train in all weather conditions, as you will be faced with this in competition.

Always lift weights with other people for your own safety. Never be afraid to ask advice from a top class thrower, but make sure they are in a good mood first!

Most important of all, *enjoy* throwing the discus.

GRAHAM SAVORY IN TRAINING

Graham at the end of the 'wind-up'   Into the first phase of the rotational run across the circle

Good knee pick-up; moving into a power-position for the throw. The discus is well to the rear

The front leg has landed to act as a block to the powerful throwing action of leg-thigh-hip

The discus trails the shoulder, with the throwing arm straight

Note the balance in Graham's position

The completion of the throw: the athlete follows through, but keeps within the circle

DAVID OTTLEY

David Ottley, 1984 Olympic silver medallist at javelin and 1986 Commonwealth champion

Javelin

Great Britain's single most successful athletic event in the 1984 Olympic Games was the Javelin. Gold, Silver and Bronze were won by the combined efforts of the men and women.

Fatima Whitbread (UK), 1987 World Champion,, European champion and Commonwealth record holder

TECHNIQUE

The Grip

There are three main methods of gripping a javelin: The Horseshoe grip, The Second Finger and Thumb Grip, and The Index Finger and Thumb Grip. It is recommended that the beginner persevere with the first two grips, as they allow the javelin to settle more naturally down the palm of the hand. Whatever your choice, the binding must be held firmly on either side of the grip ledge in order to prevent slipping when executing the throw.

The Nine-Stride Approach

This is written from the right-handed thrower's point of view. If you are left-handed, simply reverse the terms.

Many top javelin throwers use a short approach run, and in the early learning stages you will find improvement easier if you throw off only a few strides. The run up explained here can be broken down into seven different components. These are as follows:

THE PRE-RUNNING STANCE

Stand facing in the direction of the throw with feet together. Hold the javelin above the right shoulder with elbow pointing forward; the grip should be in line with the top of your head, the javelin's point a little lower than the rest of the javelin. Fix your eyes on a target just above the horizon and try to keep them there until you have completed the throw.

THE CARRY

Start your run-up with your left leg. Increase speed over these first few strides smoothly and stay relaxed. As you run, think of staying tall. Control the javelin's movements, trying to keep the arm and javelin in the same position as described above.

THE WITHDRAWAL

When your right foot touches the ground on the fourth step, withdraw the javelin back smoothly over the right shoulder, until the arm is straight. Keep the javelin in line with the direction of the throw. Make sure that your right palm is facing the sky, and that the point of the javelin is seen close to your head and just above your eyeline. Your chest should be facing to the right, but your eyes must be looking forward.

MOVING WITH THE JAVELIN WITHDRAWN

With the javelin withdrawn, the hips will naturally work to face slightly to your right, so let them do so. Each stride taken now *must* be energetic and increasing in speed. Allow your free left arm to assist the increase of speed by letting it move in a high cross body-sweeping action, in opposite reaction to your right leg. If your javelin touches the ground while in this phase, then your arm is too low.

THE CROSS-OVER STRIDE

The cross-over or pre-throw stride is of vital importance, as it allows the thrower to land in the correct throwing position before unleashing the javelin. When the left foot lands on the seventh stride, the cross-over begins and the left leg should immediately claw back the ground, keeping the momentum going. As the right knee drives through high, the left arm should be wrapped across the body, remaining there until the throw begins. On leaving the ground, the feeling you should experience is that of a delay. The right foot will now be ahead of the body and must be allowed to land when it is ready. Do not claw back the leg in an attempt to reach for the ground. When it lands, you will be in a lean-back position, ready to throw.

THE THROW

Make sure that when the right foot lands the hips stay high, thereby preventing a weak sitting position from occurring. The initial movement is derived from the right leg and hip thrusting forward, which is closely followed by the chest and right shoulder. As this occurs, make the left arm active by pulling it *fast across* the body to the left. When the left foot has landed the classic 'bow' position will be the result, creating the torque needed for good javelin throwing.

Throughout this phase, the right arm should be 'left behind', relaxed, primed

Tessa Sanderson (UK), 1984 Olympic champion

THE RECOVERY

After releasing the javelin, the follow-through will require you to allow between 1½ and 2 metres' clearance from your left foot to the scratch line. This is to prevent the recovery stride from fouling the throw.

When the right recovery foot lands, you will find yourself facing the direction of the throw with your eyes following the flight of the javelin.

Measuring your run-up

Stand on the scratch line and, without your javelin, run away from the normal direction of throwing, simulating the approach run and throw. Leave a check mark 30 cms further than your recovery foot.

and ready to throw. From now on, concentrate on keeping the left side of the body firm and throwing high over the right shoulder. Finally, think of your hand chasing the javelin until it is released.

To be a successful javelin thrower, you do not necessarily have to be either exceptionally large or small in stature. The type of athlete who propels today's javelin to new records is a multi-talented person usually capable of respectable decathlon or heptathlon scores. The reason for this is that the javelin thrower requires speed and acceleration on the run up, followed by a dynamic coordinated full body action to thrust the implement into the air.

TRAINING

Warm up and mobility

The potential of a javelin thrower can be sadly limited if he or she is not willing to spend time on mobility. Before every training session an athlete must warm up, and in the case of a javelin thrower must also incorporate mobility exercises. Parts of the body which require the greatest attention are the shoulders, back and hips. It would be advisable to spend some extra time each day on mobility exercises if you are particularly stiff in these areas. Some people find stretching dull: if you are one of these, why not join a music mobility class?

Technique training

Attempting to throw off a full approach before practising technique drills is like driving a Formula One in a Grand Prix before mastering a Mini Metro in town: disastrous! It is therefore vital that technique exercises are practised conscientiously in order to drill in correct body movements which can be transferred on to a full approach. Here are a few to practise.

THE STANDING THROW
(For the right-handed thrower.) Starting with body weight over the right foot, perform a throw as described in the previous section on this (see p.128). Concentrate on technique: do not try to achieve personal bests on each effort.

THE FIVE-STRIDE THROW
Stand with the javelin withdrawn. Begin with the left foot first and perform the technique described on p. 128 in the previous section. Ensure that you accelerate smoothly with this practice, being careful not to lean forward when trying to gain momentum.

RUNNING AND CROSS-OVER DRILLS
Learning to relax while running with a javelin in the correct position can be assisted by two main drills. First, practice the carrying position as explained on p. 128 for 20 – 30 minutes. Second, withdraw and run with the javelin behind you for a similar distance. Concentrate on the left leg clawing back and the right knee picking up as indicated under 'The Cross-over Stride' on p. 128.

If it is safe, then finish each running drill by going through the motions of a throw.

Medicine ball training

Many schools and sport centres have old medicine balls hidden in their stores, discarded as an outmoded method of physical training by the less well informed. If you are able to find and use one of them, then there are many exercises useful to a javelin thrower which you can do. Here are a few to try.

Standing forward throw. Grasp the ball in front of the body with both hands. Bend your knees, with the ball hanging down, and throw it forward for distance.

Standing overhead throw. Stand with feet about shoulder-width apart. Grasp the ball in front of you with both hands. Bend your knees, then throw the ball back over your head for distance (watch out for light fittings with this one!).

Lying down throw. i.e on your back and, stretching your arms above your head, grasp the ball. With straight arms, throw the ball past your feet for distance.

Standing football throw. With feet together, or apart, and the ball grasped firmly with straight arms above your head, throw forward for distance. This exercise can also be performed off a 3- or 5-stride approach.

Try to work with a partner, on these exercises, throwing back and forward, and do at least fifty throws per session with a 1½ – 3-kilo ball.

Basic strength and weight training

Initially a novice thrower should gain basic strength from 'safe' body weight exercises such as press-ups, dips, sit-ups, burpees, pull-ups etc. These exercises can be performed as part of a circuit in any gymnasium, or with a little imagination in the case of pull-ups, in the home.

If the circuits you have devised become easy after a while, then make it harder by increasing sets and repetitions or decreasing recovery time. A typical circuit might read as follows:

Press-ups	3 sets×8 repetitions with ½ minute rest between sets and repetitions
Sit-ups	3 sets×8 repetitions, ½ minute rest as before
Burpees	3 sets×8 repetitions, ½ minute rest as before
Dips	3 sets×8 repetitions, ½ minute rest as before
Squat jumps	3 sets×8 repetitions, ½ minute rest as before

Once the foundations of basic strength have been laid, then you can slowly introduce weight-training sessions. Basic weight training exercises such as bench press, squats, snatch, jerks and sit-ups are all of benefit to javelin throwers. In addition to these, more specific exercises (such as variations on bent and straight-arm pullovers using barbells, dumbells and differing inclines) and trunk-twisting exercises must be incorporated into your routine. A typical weight training session may read:

Snatch 3 sets×6 repetitions
Bench Press 3×6
Squat 3×6
Trunk twists 3×6 each way
Incline straight arm pullovers 3×6

With weight training, I recommend strongly that you go to a popular weight training area, and get advice on correct lifting techniques and safety procedures from the very start. Don't risk having an accident or wasting effort by performing the exercises incorrectly.

DAVID OTTLEY IN TRAINING

Preparation for the approach run

David runs aggressively but relaxed, with good knee lift

Withdrawal of the javelin: hips are still forward as David continues his run

David gathers himself ready for the throw

David adopts a wide stance over which to apply force to the javelin. The front locked leg braces the body as the arm begins to pull the javelin through

Starting the cross-over, preparatory to the throwing position. The javelin is still held back

The throw is completed, with a final leg reverse to keep David behind the line

DAVID SMITH

David Smith is the 1986 Commonwealth Games hammer champion, and English record-holder

The Hammer

The hammer event is of Celtic origin, deriving from country fairs where sledge hammers were thrown. By the mid 1800s a round ball on a wooden shaft evolved, which is still in use today in most Highland Games events.

At the 1900 Olympics in Paris, the wooden shaft had been changed to a wire with a handle. The circle, nine feet in diameter, was reduced to seven feet (2.15 m) after these games. The event in the early years of this century was dominated by strongmen of Irish American descent, who used their great strength to bully the hammer. The 1936 Olympics saw the rise of the more athletic thrower who, by completing three continuous turns on a 'cinder' circle, produced the winning throw. This technique is the forerunner of a fast continuous rotation over a three- or four-turn throw, which is now largely dominated by Eastern European athletes.

TECHNIQUE

This is an event that demands a particular precision: you must master its component parts before you can combine everything into throwing a hammer. The following is based on a right-handed thrower turning anti-clockwise. The glove is worn on the left hand, with the fingers placed through the handle: the right hand is placed on top of the glove to grip the hand safely.

Before throwing, an athlete must **always make sure the area is safe and free of people.**

The swings

Take your position inside the cage with your back facing the direction of the throw. The hammer head should be placed off the right foot. The hammer is then raised off the ground to pass behind the head, forming a nice easy arc. It should reach a high point at 6 o'clock, directly behind the head, and a low point at 12 o'clock, in front of the body between the feet. This should form an easy circular path at 45 degrees to the ground, and not a near-vertical path like a windmill.

When you are competent with the swings, practise the standing throw. Complete two or three easy swings and then release the hammer as it rises towards 6 o'clock.

The turn

The turn is a continuous smooth motion which is initiated by the feet, and not by the shoulders pulling away (which will cause a jerky throw). You should learn this *without* using a hammer.

Stand in the same position as for the swings, with knees slightly bent and your body upright. Turn 180 degrees on the heel of your left foot and the ball of your right. The right knee should be tight in behind the left knee, as the closer the knees are at this point, the shorter the distance travelled by the right foot in the second half of the turn. The right foot is raised as the thrower turns slightly on the ball of the left foot, and then placed to bring your shoulders, hips, knees and feet in line, facing towards 3 o'clock: turn on both toes to complete the whole turn.

When multiples of turns can be completed without thinking where your feet are to be placed, you can start turning using a hammer. At first, practise continuous turns at a very slow speed to get the feeling of the body and feet turning as a unit. The arms should be relaxed as the hammer rises from the low to the high point. Providing the right knee is turned in tight behind the left knee, the right foot can then be placed down nice and early, at the 3 o'clock position. Keeping your sense of your body as a unit, and your actions to match, i.e. shoulders, hips and feet in line, the right foot is then screwed into the ground without letting the shoulders get in front of the hammer – this is the acceleration phase. Once the hammer head passes 12 o'clock the unit must become passive again and let the hammer rise to its high point. If at any point in the turn you could draw lines out from the end of each foot, they would be near-parallel.

When you can turn slowly, keeping shoulders in line with hips and feet, the system can then be allowed to accelerate naturally. A common problem at this stage is allowing the head and left shoulder to pull away at the beginning of each turn, which causes the thrower to land heavily on the right foot throughout the throw. If this happens to you, you must work to overcome it.

Easy throws may now be practised by starting very slowly, allowing the rhythm to build into each turn by being passive on the left and working progressively harder on an early right foot. Take care when practising this drill to observe strict positioning of the feet: don't allow bodyweight to fall on to the right foot. This foot should be placed in position while maintaining long rangy shoulders and an upright body position on bent legs. The thrower should never enter a pike position (body leaning forward and bottom stuck out).

A useful drill to improve balance and the turning action of the right foot is to turn starting and finishing at 6 o'clock, or 180 degrees. Turns should be practiced without the hammer: use the high point as your focal point. Complete half a turn so you are facing 6 o'clock. The right foot is placed down at 3 o'clock, and once down it does not stop turning until it is facing 6 o'clock. Keep the left foot parallel to the right at all times, and maintain the body's upright position with legs bent.

Once you have pulled all these component parts together, and mastered the technique necessary to throw the hammer, you will start working on perfecting your action and throwing longer and longer distances. But, as with all events, you cannot neglect the groundwork: you must have an effective training programme.

Sergey Litvinov (USSR), world champion 1983 and 1987

WEIGHT LIFTING

Weight lifting is an important part of a hammer thrower's training. A preferred system gives a method of periodization where maximum singles are never practiced. All the exercises are based on four sets, i.e.:

4 sets×8 reps; 4×6; 4×5; 4×4

The bar will ascend in weight from first to last set. One or two sets should be practised beforehand to give the body a good warm-up prior to doing the maximum lifts, e.g.:

Power cleans (4×4):
4×80 kg: 4×100 kg (warm up)
4×120 kg: 4×130 kg: 4×140 kg: 4×150 kg

Martin Girvan, UK record holder,
Commonwealth silver medallist 1982 and 1986

WINTER TRAINING PROGRAMME

The following is an example of the sort of training you should undertake in the winter.

MONDAY
Warm up
High pulls (snatch grip)
Power cleans
Press behind neck
Upright rowing
Squats
Bench press
Lat pulls
Abdominals
Warm down

WEDNESDAY
Warm up
Narrow grip snatch
Dead lifts
Bent-over rowing
Leg curls
Leg extensions
Hyper extensions

FRIDAY
Warm up
High pulls (clean grip)
Power snatch
Press in front
Front squats
Bench press
Lats
Abdominals

Fast and aggressive in the circle, Yuriy Sedykh (USSR), Olympic champion 1976 and 1980, and six times world record holder

This programme may be used in the sets where 4 × 6 reps are being used. Also during the winter the hammer thrower should undertake short dynamic sprints of 60 m. He should also indulge in competitive games, with other athletes who are training, such as overhead shot, standing long jump and any competitions that can be devised. Mentally, over the winter period, you are aiming to build up the will to win.

During the competitive summer season the emphasis is on technique work and strength training. You should not neglect sprinting.

These are guidelines to improve your balance, rhythm and acceleration. A good technique is of paramount importance. There is far too much emphasis on strength in British throwing: technique will, at the end of the day, beat the strongman.

DAVID SMITH THROWS THE HAMMER

Starting position, showing the grip

Beginning the swing: the hammer is rising close to the high point. The hips counter-balance the action

Note the arms are bent and the hands are pressing over the front of the head

The second turn. The arms are long and in line with the hips and the head. The hammer passes through the low point: technique ensures that this does not pull at the left shoulder, which could throw an athlete off balance. The arms continue to be passive, the right leg turns close to facilitate early lift, and the hips are now counter-balancing the increasing pull of the hammer

The beginning of the delivery. The right foot lands

The hammer passes the low point off the left foot. The left side of the body begins to block and the legs start to drive as the hammer rises

The hammer descends: the angle of the left moves from 90° to 180°, and the right arm straightens with it at the beginning of the entry, into the first turn

The body swings into the circle with the hammer remaining low. The hammer then rises again towards the high point: the arms are passive; the right leg is turned in close

The right foot comes down early. Head, hips and knees are all in line (above left). This is the third turn: the hammer passes through the low point again, and then rises as David spins into the fourth turn on his left foot. The head, body and hips are all acting as one unit

With the left foot fixed, the hammer is released. David's technique is the result of twelve years' hard work

Part Five: The Decathlon

EUGENE GILKES

Eugene Gilks is a former European Junior silver medallist for the 4×400 m relay. He is currently ranked as the third best British decathlete in history, with 7,889 points.

The decathlon has always been at some distance from the centre stage of British athletics. Until the latter part of the 1970s it was largely unknown to the viewing public. And those who were aware of its existence were offered too little by way of media coverage to allow a sufficient understanding of its complex nature, leaving them with a generally negative view of the event. But ten years on, and much has changed. Surely there is no Briton who does not know the name Daley Thompson, the world's greatest all-round athlete and the current world record holder in the decathlon.

The decathlon is the supreme test of athletic ability and versatility, and the road to excellence is long and arduous. Our young hopefuls must be encouraged and supported as they discover and ultimately conquer the physical and mental challenges imposed by the event. Only then will another British world-beater emerge.

WHAT IS THE DECATHLON?

The decathlon consists of ten disciplines contested over two days, five on each day.

FIRST DAY
100 m
long jump
shot put
high jump
400 m

SECOND DAY
110 m hurdles
discus throw
pole vault
javelin
1500 m

The disciplines are always executed in the same order.

1984 Olympic silver medallist and former world record holder Jurgen Hingsten (FRG) in the pole vault

1972 Olympic pentathlon champion Mary Peters (UK)

There is generally an allowance of at least thirty minutes between the end of one event and the beginning of another. However, there is no maximum interim period. It is therefore theoretically possible for the five disciplines to span the entire day. In practice this only occurs when there are an excessive number of competitors, or when other events have to be programmed into a day's activities, as happens at major championships.

There are certain rules that are unique to the decathlon. These are:

1 A competitor is disqualified after three false starts (not two as in individual events).

2 In the long jump and the throwing disciplines, only three trials are permitted (as opposed to six in individual events).

3 A record in the event will not be permitted if the wind speed in one or more disciplines is in excess of 4m per second (not 2m as in individual events). With the exception of major championships, the organizers of a decathlon will, where possible, try to give the benefit of wind-speed factors to the competitors.

4 The decathlon is based on a points scoring system taken from the 1985 IAAF scoring tables. Every performance has a corresponding score and the overall winner is determined by the man who accumulates the highest points total over the ten events.

5 If a decathlete does not finish a race, or has no successful throws or jumps, he will not register a score in that particular discipline.

6 If a decathlete fails to attempt a trial in any one discipline, he will not be permitted to take any further part in the decathlon competition.

THE NATURE OF THE DECATHLON

It is the emphasis on all-round excellence that makes the decathlon physically and psychologically unique. The decathlete must, in the first place, compete against themself, conquering physical and mental inadequacies, using the event as an adversary and the points table as a weapon. Only then can the challenge of the other competitors be considered.

Consistency

The event requires consistency of performance. It should be noted that the difference between a good and a world-class decathlete is that the former's weak events are usually diabolical, whereas the latter's verge on international standard. It is therefore necessary to remember that decathlons are **never** won on one or two outstanding events, but **are** lost because of the weak ones. The consistent performer can go through a decathlon without a single win and still finish the eventual victor.

Think . . . but not too much!

It is the mental rather than the physical stress that makes a decathlon such a demanding event. The all-round performer will compete for their club on a Saturday afternoon in six or seven events with a couple of relays at the end for good measure, all in the space of three hours. In such circumstances, you can't possibly concentrate on the individual demands of each event. You just relax, enjoy yourself and do them. If you mess up your long jump there isn't time to worry about it, because your name is simultaneously being called from both ends of the track for the start of the 100 m, *and* your second putt in the shot.

But a certain level of concentration must be maintained *throughout* the competition, which can last for as long as twelve hours on each day. The athlete must be as mentally sharp for his last event as for his first. The development of this mental discipline must not be neglected.

HOW TO GET STARTED

Tracking down a decathlon coach is a lot more difficult than it sounds. They are a rare species. If you have access to a club, they may have a coach with experience in multi-events. If not they are likely to know of someone in your area who does.

If you are unable to make contact with anyone who can advise you, write to:

The British Amateur Athletics Board Coaching Office
Francis House
Francis Street
London SW1

or write to the AAA in your county (see page 160).

I am sure you will find them most helpful in this respect.

Join a club . . .

It will be important for you to join an athletic club. It can provide you with a friendly and stimulating training environment, offering not only a track but also the use of equipment: javelin, shots, hurdles, etc. It also gives you the opportunity to compete in your events outside the decathlon situation. Where possible do try to work with a group, preferably of decathletes. Your decathlon coach may very well have a group of his own. So much the better! It is so important that you get yourself into a relaxed training atmosphere, because if you are happy you will train harder and learn quicker.

All the right gear

You will naturally want to keep your initial outlay to a minimum. I would recommend the following list as the barest essentials for getting started in training:

Training shoes
Sprinting spikes
A track/jog suit
Shorts
Vests
Socks
T-shirts
An old pullover
A showerproof anorak.

Most of these items I am sure you will already possess. That being the case, the only real expense will be the sprinting spikes.

SO WHAT ABOUT THIS TRAINING?

The coach decides the programme. He will choose the emphases and priorities. There is no right or wrong way of coaching a particular discipline: aptitudes differ and training must therefore be adapted to the individual.

Technical skills

The correct and sound acquisition of technical skills cannot be emphasized enough. Good scores are possible with poor techniques, but in carrying such deficiencies you sacrifice the chance of a *great* score. Once the correct techniques are ground in, you have a sound base on which to build. They should be simple, efficient and effective. It is only then that you should begin to think about intricacies.

But remember, you won't master things in a week. It takes a little longer. It is a step-by-step progression. So be patient.

Try not to be drawn to working on only the events you like. They are usually your best, and not the ones that need the work.

Running speed is a key factor in decathlon. It is the basis of six of the ten disciplines and should therefore be developed as part of the solid foundation on which to build a great score.

The technical events generally requiring the most work will be the pole vault, hurdles and javelin. So, the earlier the work is begun on these the quicker the very involved skills will be developed.

Most decathletes use weight training as part of their strength and power development. This is one aspect of a programme in which it is easy to become over-zealous, especially during the winter months. However, **be warned**, the build-up of excessive and unnecessary muscle bulk will inevitably adversely effect mobility, the endurance potential and the basic power/weight ratio of the body.

1500 M . . . CAN YOU WIN?

Many decathletes tend to neglect the 1500 m in training. This is **not** a good idea! Although the least loved it is still one of the ten decathlon disciplines. It is just plain stupid to throw away points on the final event, having worked so hard over the first nine.

Beware that excessive endurance work can have a negative effect on your basic speed. If you have an area of woodland in your neighbourhood you will probably find a couple of steady runs per week quite adequate.

HOW LONG . . . HOW OFTEN?

Training time and frequency is something that must be decided between you and your coach when all the relevant factors have been taken into consideration. It is, however, advisable not to overdo a training programme in intensity, especially in the early stages. Sufficient rest periods should be provided between sessions allowing the body to recuperate entirely. This should reduce the possibility of fatigue-induced injury.

Once you have started your training programme you will find that your initial progress will be swift. However, there is then likely to be a levelling-off period. This is how your development will be; there will be times, often long in duration, when little progress is being made. This is when your motivation is put to the test. You must be patient and persevere.

One of the all-time great athletes: double Olympic, one World, double European and triple Commonwealth champion Daley Thompson finishing the 1500 m, the decathlon's last event, in the Moscow Olympics 1980

THE COMPETITION

The object over the two days is to remain warm and dry, thus allowing you to perform at your best. My suggestions with the emphasis once again on minimizing the cost, are as follows:

Jogging suits (2 pairs)
Training shoes (2 pairs)
Spikes (2 pairs)
Socks (4 pairs)
Shorts (2 pairs)
Vests (2)
T-shirts (3)
Plenty of warm clothing, such as pullovers
A sleeping bag or blankets to help stay warm between events
Large plastic bags in which to place clothing in the very likely event of rain
A woolly hat will greatly reduce heat loss

In addition:
Hot and cold snacks
Tape/talcum powder
Venison turps/lighter fuel
Spike spanners and spare spikes
Towels

Get warm . . . stay warm

You should start each day with a long and thorough warm-up. For the rest of the day heat can be best conserved by staying dry, and wearing plenty of warm clothes. You thus require only a relatively short time to be ready for each subsequent event.

THE EVENT

For those of you who may have elected to tackle the event without the advice or guidance of a coach, I would like to offer some very rough guidelines. They key phrase is 'Play it safe and keep it simple.'

The 100 m is fairly straight forward; just try to relax and go go go! The 400 m on the other hand will require a little more judgement of pace. But always remember that it will be the end of the first day and you have a whole night to recover. So commit yourself.

For the long jump and three throws the strategies are similar. With only three trials it is vitally important that the first is made to count. So a safe controlled first attempt registering a score (e.g. a standing throw), will allow a more committed second attempt. Then hopefully your third will be your best.

In the high jump and pole vault, come into the competition at a height *you know you can clear*. This will serve two purposes – primarily it will register a score, but also it will give you an opportunity to test your run up and warm yourself up for the higher, more risky heights.

Being the first event on the second day, the importance of a good run in the hurdles is obvious. As in the 100 m or 400 m

149

you must commit yourself, although for the novice this could prove a rather painful and destructive experience! If you are totally new to the discipline and have trouble maintaining three strides between the flights it might be an idea to try five before graduating to three.

I have always found it useful – certainly in my earlier days – to place some kind of padding (perhaps a folded handkerchief), over the trailing leg ankle bone. This should help ease some of the pain, but I'm sorry . . . it won't improve your time!

While it is true the 1500m is an event liked by nobody, it is the tenth and final discipline and must be completed. Don't fear it – do it! If you allow thoughts of it to start dominating you, it will have a hold forever. Pace yourself safely and you will find it a lot easier than you think.

Friendly . . . but not too friendly

The decathlon is perhaps the friendliest event in track and field athletics. However, don't make the mistake of getting caught up in the camaraderie and thereby lose your concentration. Never lose sight of your final goal!

In the same way preoccupation with the points table, trying to keep up with a prior and probably outlandish prediction of scores, can also be counterproductive with respect to your concentration level. If you really must set yourself targets, try to

Daley Thompson in action

make them realistic. The only score that really matters is the final one.

I do not propose to suggest a target score. I believe that at the beginning of your decathlon career you should compete to enjoy and finish the event. Don't expect unreasonable things of yourself. If you keep improving on subsequent scores you are succeeding!

SO YOU WANT TO BE THE BEST

After a relatively short period, whether or not you have what it takes to make it to the very top will become abundantly clear. If you have world-class potential and you have no doubts that it is what you really want, then now is the time that you must commit yourself. The decathlon must become your way of life – a state of mind. Sacrifices must be made.

The simple things that you have always taken for granted are now of the utmost importance; nutrition, balanced and regular sleep patterns.

You must look to cementing your self-motivation, to further developing speed, strength, fitness and flexibility. You must school your mind. You and your coach will need to organize for yourself the medical back-up, so that you know you have access to a physiotherapist if you need one – something athletes in so many other countries take for granted.

You must be prepared to live, breathe, sleep and eat the decathlon.

Consideration will need to be given from a technical point of view to perhaps seeing specialist coaches for your individual disciplines. That too is a decision that you and your decathlon coach must make together.

DRUG ABUSE

On your way to the top there is something that will keep 'popping up' – drug abuse.

In some countries it appears to be the norm, and in Britain it is not unknown. While it is true that an earnest effort appears to be being made in an attempt to stamp out this deplorable abuse, I fear it will be with us for some time yet.

If you really want to be the best there is no place in your list of equipment for anything of this nature now or ever. The moment you join the abusers . . . you have already lost!

IN CONCLUSION

Combined-events performers are athletes in the truest sense. The decathlon is sometimes rejected by fine young athletes in Britain, perhaps as being the 'soft option'. The answer to that is – you try it!

The decathlon is an event of which you will never tire. Its diversity will ensure you are never bored. Its complexity will ensure you are always tested, always striving . . . Each decathlon you do will have its own successes and disappointments. From every one, you will learn something new about the event and about yourself. As the supreme test, its satisfactions are hard to beat.

Part Six: Tips From The Top

FATIMA WHITBREAD

1987 world champion; 1986 European champion and Commonwealth record holder

1 Develop a working and understanding relationship with a coach. Make your discussions a two-way situation where you pool your competitive experience with their technical expertise.

2 Believe in yourself without being conceited. If you do not believe in yourself, who will?

3 Remember that you meet the same people on the way down as you passed on the way up. Always treat people in the manner in which you would like them to treat you.

4 Choose your friends carefully. Real friendship is precious. The truth is revealed when you are in trouble and it is then that you discover your true friends.

5 Remember you are only as good as your next competition. Unlike some other sports, you cannot talk a good performance.

JACK BUCKNER

1986 European 5000 m champion and 1987 World bronze medallist

1 Enjoy athletics when you are young. It is far better to *undertrain* as a teenager than to overtrain. Don't take the sport too seriously at an early age.

2 In training it is important to aim for consistency. It is preferable to train steadily and regularly over several months rather than to train very hard for a couple of weeks and then feel too exhausted to maintain training over the next few weeks.

3 I always find that it is better to train on grass rather than on roads. In my experience, injuries are frequently caused by over-use and stress. Running on grass minimizes the risk of these injuries.

4 Always be prepared to learn from others and be receptive to information on all aspects of the sport. There are countless training tips to be learnt by listening to athletes, coaches and physiotherapists.

5 Do not expect instant improvement from training. Be patient, as hard training can take months before the deserved results are achieved.

ALAN PASCOE

Former European and Commonwealth champion at 400 m hurdles

1 Find a good, qualified coach early on and enter into a planned, well-organized training programme. Enjoyment of athletics doesn't mean that you shouldn't TAKE IT SERIOUSLY.

2 Don't neglect the rest periods between training sessions. Over-training can lead to physical stress and injury. You must allow your body to recuperate properly before embarking on another hard session.

3 A hurdler can enjoy a number of events. To be successful he must have sprint speed, so if you are good enough run in sprints and relays. You will find that competing at other events is very relaxing and does not have the anxiety of competing at your main event.

ROGER BLACK

1986 European 400 m champion

1   Train in a friendly group environment under a coach so that there will be a purpose to your work.

2   During competition try to relax. The essence of the good competitor, especially in 400 m running, is to run with speed and relaxation.

3   Too many athletes only give 80% because they know how much 100% will hurt. Learn to run through the so called 'pain barrier' in training and racing – the sweet smell of success is on the other side!

MICHAEL McFARLANE

1982 Commonwealth 200 m champion, finalist in 1984 Olympic Games 100 m

1 Enjoy your athletics. Do what suits you as a person. Try a number of events to find which you are best at.

2 When you have made up your mind that you want to be one of the best, find a good coach, fully commit yourself and embark on a long-term programme.

3 Remember that you will not be number one all the time, so be graceful in defeat. Everybody has their ups and downs – learn to cope with them and don't let the downs get you down!

ZOLA BUDD

Twice winner of the world cross championships and winner of the 1985 European Cup 3000 m in Moscow

1 Run for yourself. It is important that you run because *you* want to run, not because a parent or coach wants it.

2 Set yourself goals, both short-term and long-term. Without targets your athletics can become an aimless affair.

3 Enjoyment of your sport is the most important thing. Even if you get to the highest level you must not lose your love of the event, or let its importance in your life diminish. Once the enjoyment has gone it is probably time to stop.

ADDRESSES

Amateur Athletic Association,
Francis House,
Francis Street,
London SW1P 1DL

Northern Ireland Amateur Athletic
Association,
House of Sport,
Upper Malone Road,
Belfast BT5 9LA

Scottish Amateur Athletic Association,
18 Ainslie Place,
Edinburgh EH3 6AU

Welsh Amateur Athletic Association,
Swansea Stadium,
Upper Bank,
Landore,
Swansea SA1 7DF

Information regarding tennis in Australia
may be obtained from:

Australian Athletic Union,
PO Box 254,
Moonee Ponds,
Melbourne,
Victoria 3030

in New Zealand:

New Zealand Amateur Athletic Association,
PO Box 741,
Wellington

in Canada:

Canadian Track and Field Association,
355 River Road,
Tower B,
Vanier City,
Ottawa,
Ontario K1L 8CI

other countries:

International Amateur Athletic Federation,
3 Hans Crescent,
Knightsbridge,
London SW1X 0LN

First published 1988 by Pan Books Ltd,
Cavaye Place, London SW10 9PG
9 8 7 6 5 4 3 2 1
© The Amateur Athletic Association 1987
Photographs by Mark Shearman
Photographs © Mark Shearman 1987
Designer: Peter Ward

ISBN 0 330 29713 9

Photoset by Parker Typesetting Service, Leicester
Printed by Richard Clay (Chichester) Ltd